## Editors' and Readers' Comments

*To Tove "the Dove" Enjoy! Marie Sadro*

"In *Erika*, your book of autobiographical stories of wartime Berlin. I particularly enjoy your imagery and diction when you describe a scenery or character. It helps me grasp your environment and your mood as well as the mood of the people around you. You have a unique sentence structure, which makes the stories genuine and very believable. As I read your stories I often felt I was standing next to you, observing the events unfolding around me as you described them.

The stories repeat details which permit them to be read out of order. I think that readers however, will read the stories in order because the series are clearly chronological and more suspenseful and interesting that way...

I also appreciate how frank, honest and yet forgiving and generous you are in your portrayal of family members. For instance, I appreciate your frankness about your father and how he could be cold, aggressive and difficult, but how this was attributed to the pressures of war and his fear for the welfare of his family. Your mother is portrayed as a fairy-like, beautiful and demure individual, somewhat naive because of her youth, while your Auntie is clearly a strong and militant woman..."

--Elicia Prystay, **University of Toronto**

The stories show the forgivable, comprehensible aspects of the war as seen through the eyes of a child ...This gives them a unique and endearing quality.

**--Tim Lashrafi**

"I loved your book. Thank you! I had to cry a few times too, it was so moving."

**--Gita K., Pforzheim, Germany**

"Excellent! Is there a sequel?"

**--Father Joe Strohhofer, Gravelbourg, Saskatchewan**

" A truly German story my children will enjoy  Can you add on your poems, pictures and recipes ?"

**--Patricia Johnson, Gold Coast, Austalia**

# ERIKA

---

## *STORIES*

## MARIE SADRO

To Tim and my children

Cover design by **Ares Jun**
Formatting and layout provided by **Quantum Formatting Service**
http://quantumformatting.weebly.com

# CONTENTS

*"Mankind must put an end to war before war puts an end to mankind."*

*John F. Kennedy*

# Open Houses

*Berlin, 1942.*

Our races to the bunkers became a nightly event. The darkness of the city, the ominous wail of sirens, the hectic surge of people, mostly women and children, through the black streets remain confused in my memory. The dive of planes with thundering engines and frightful incendiary bombs, which supposedly fell out of the sky like candles on a Christmas tree, are blocked out of my mind. I believe I closed my eyes as I hung on to Auntie's rough knuckles and ran mutely by her side down the Kurfuerstendam towards the air raid shelters. I remember no particular explosion, air raid or fire bomb although I am told that I experienced them almost nightly when I was three and four years old.

What I remember vividly is our frenzied haste whenever the sirens began to howl. My father's aunt, whom we called Auntie, said that her dentures came lose and rattled whenever she heard the alarm. My mother blushed and trembled with nervous excitement. Her blond tendrils clung to her moist forehead while her large blue eyes were dilated with fear. I do not remember the reaction of my father, the doctor, although he was with us at the time. His subdued manly terror was lost in the frenzy of women trying to salvage valuables in case our dwelling would be struck that night.

I recall especially our exit from the bunkers in the grey, often rainy dawn, when all was quiet and people crept about like eerie shadows deprived of sensation because of the terror and losses they had experienced that night.

But I was not afraid. I was brave and even amused as I looked at the devastation around me: the charred houses, the palls of smoke, the tumbled down walls whose stones and rubble littered the streets. I had survived the night. It was going to be another fun day with toys and games. I teased my little brother Joey in anticipation. He was only three and I was four and so much wiser than he. Auntie walked us back to our apartment while my mother and father headed home ahead of us with my twin baby sisters.

I observed the massive apartment houses deprived of their outer walls, their fine interiors and luxurious furniture exposed indecently to public view. Auntie, who had grown up in the poverty of the Depression and harbored a secret hatred towards the rich, joined us in our merriment. We were happy to be alive and return to our unscathed home.

"Look at the beautiful sofa hanging half way over the wall," I laughed as I pointed to the upper floor of a damaged building. "We can see their beds! Auntie, are the people going to sleep there tonight?" I tugged at her hand. "Can we come and watch them have supper and go to bed?"

"You are silly, Erika," she said. "People can't live in houses without walls."

"Why not? Their furniture is there. If they turn on their stove, they will be warm."

"I don't think so. They'll come and get their furniture and live somewhere else," she said.

"Can we go inside and look?" I asked.

"No," she replied.

I kept on babbling in my childish way. It seemed to me that this building without a façade would be great fun. It was not even black and charred like most of the houses. It looked normal except that its front wall had crumbled away.

"Why can't we go in?" I persisted. "We could get the toys. The people won't mind if we get their toys. Perhaps the children are dead and won't need them anymore. There might be a toy train for Joey."

When Joey heard the word "train," he got very excited. "I want a train! I want a train!" he cried and stamped his feet.

Auntie hesitated. The door was blown away. No one was in sight. The building looked solid enough with stairs and railings. Only the outer wall was almost entirely ripped off. The upper floor was slanted and the roof was gone so that the attic stairs led to nowhere.

"Couldn't we go in, just a little bit?" I begged.

"I don't think it is safe for children," she said. "But if you stay on the sidewalk where I can see you, I will peek in to see if someone needs help."

I saw that curiosity had gotten the better of her. She asked me to hold Joey's hand, not to budge, and, especially, not to talk to anyone. "I won't be long," she added.

"How long will you be?"

"Remember the song I sing you at night, *Guten Abend, gute Nacht*? Well, if you sing that song softly, I'll be back before you're finished."

She also told me not to sing too fast.

I stayed on the sidewalk and held my little brother's hand and sang Brahm's lullaby while my aunt walked between the door jambs as if she was walking into a picture frame. I watched her test the steps carefully with her feet, then go up resolutely and disappear around a landing.

I soon finished the song and waited for my aunt to come down the stairs. But she did not appear. I looked up at the naked building, but could not see her in any of the rooms. She liked golden necklaces and earrings. May be she had found a treasure chest. She might even find a doll for me and a train for Joey.

Time passed. A tall haggard woman in black with disheveled hair was tottering down the street in our direction. I began to freeze. I was sure this strange woman would ask us questions if Auntie did not appear at once. I looked at the exposed stairs, but the open house had swallowed Auntie. She was not in the kitchen with its wooden chairs placed neatly around a dinner table as if waiting for their owners. She was not in the bathroom with its gleaming fixtures. Meanwhile, the tall woman had approached us. She bent down to our height, her black eyes surrounded by dark circles, burning like coals in her ashen face

"Where is your mother?" she asked in a hollow voice.

"My mother is not here," I said quickly and squeezed Joey's hand. My little brother began to wail. The woman looked disturbed.

"Who left you here?" she asked.

I did not want Auntie to get into trouble, so I did not answer.

"Come with me!" she insisted and grabbed Joey's hand and mine. "I will find your mother."

Joey, intrigued by the turn of events, stopped whimpering.

"I don't want to go with you," I protested.

"Oh, there are so many little ones separated from their parents. I am looking for my little boy. I lost him here in the terrible air raid last night. Come with me!"

"No!" I cried and tried to free my hand. Joey started to weep again.

"I won't hurt you, children!" she said. "My home is not far away. I will find your parents."

She held our hands tightly and pulled us along with long strides. I followed her with terror in my soul. I remembered the story of Hansel and Gretel. Perhaps she was a witch.

Fortunately, Auntie came out of the building. She stood on the sidewalk and looked for us. When she saw us with the strange woman, she came running after us.

"What are you doing?" she screamed at the stranger who let go of our hands.

"Are they your children?" asked the startled woman. " I lost my little boy in the darkness and the rush of the crowd last night. Did you see him?"

Her voice was pitiful and her black eyes were filled with sorrow.

"I saw no child," replied Auntie.

The woman made a sound like the moan of a wounded beast. "I must search again. I must find Johan!"

I watched her stumble down the road as if she was about to fall.

Auntie was shaken. Her hands tightened on ours as she rushed us home in the opposite direction. "People go crazy in the war," she muttered.

"Did you find a doll for me and a train for Joey?" I asked.

"Honey," she said. "I did not have the heart to touch anything. There was a dead little boy in the corner of the staircase." And I saw tears roll down her wrinkled cheeks.

*"To walk through the ruined cities of Germany is to feel an actual doubt about the continuity of civilization."*

George Orwell

# Toy Horse

A few years after the fall of the Berlin Wall in 1990, I returned to Berlin. It was my first visit to my native city since my parents had left Germany. As I was walking down the famous boulevard *Unter den Linden* towards the Brandenburg Gate, I ran into a noisy parade of young people waving colourful banners with slogans of peace and tolerance. I saw them again at the arch where they rallied with rock music and speeches. How times have changed! My family used to live near *Friedrichstrasse*. Many times we had walked *Unter den Linden*, but the Berlin of my childhood was gone. Only a few bullet scars and chipped cornices on walls reminded me of how things had been, and hopefully would never be again.

It was a little white horse on wooden wheels that could be pulled on a string. It had shiny marble eyes, a scarlet saddle and bridle, and a bushy silken tail. It looked playful and lively. But it was not my toy. It belonged to my brother Joey, who had received it for his second birthday.

The lovely little horse, which did not seem to excite Joey in the least, intrigued me immensely. I kept trying to stroke its soft mane and tail, only to be tapped on my fingers like a naughty girl. "Erika, this is Joey's toy!" scolded Auntie. "Go play with your dolly!" Auntie was my father's unmarried aunt. She lived with us and helped Mom with Joey and me.

One afternoon after our nap, Auntie prepared us for our daily walk. She felt that the stuffy air in city apartments was unhealthy and that children should get fresh air at least once a day. She helped me into my velvet coat, leather boots and felt hat and dressed my little brother in the blue woolen outfit she had knit. Because he was too young to walk on cobblestone sidewalks, she tucked him into his fashionable swan shaped stroller.

I watched her go to the closet, slip on her black coat with fur collar, pin her little black hat with netting over her coiled grey braids and pick up her leather purse and umbrella.

I pointed at the little horse perched on a dresser. "Can I take it along?"

"I told you many times. It's not yours, Erika. It's your brother's," said Auntie.

"Yes, but Joey will want to play with it. He can pull it in the park."

I turned to Joey, "You want your horsey, Joey? Say, yes! You want your pretty horsey?"

My little brother screeched and reached for the horse. He could not talk yet.

"See, Auntie, Joey wants it," I argued.

Auntie hesitated, then picked up the pull toy and put it in the stroller. "All right, we'll take it along. But we can't lose it. It is a special gift from your Opa."

Opa was my mother's father. He and Oma, our grandmother, always gave us treats when we visited them in their home in Oberschefflenz near Heidelberg.

"I'll watch very carefully that Joey doesn't lose it," I promised.

"You do that!" said Auntie.

She took the stroller in her strong arms and carried it, with Joey in it, down the long flight of stairs. We occupied the third floor of a large apartment building where my father had a medical practice on the floor below.

From the narrow street where we lived, we headed for the *Friedrichstrasse* nearby. This route would take us to the famous boulevard *Unter den Linden* and the park behind the Brandenburg Gate. We had done this walk many times before.

Auntie proceeded at a brisk martial walk, and I trotted along. There had been an air raid the night before and a neighboring district had been hit. We passed by smoldering buildings, charred houses with burnt furniture, and crumbling walls with gaping holes where windows used to be. Auntie found a path around rocks and debris and carried the stroller over piled up obstacles when there was none.

We arrived to the wide boulevard *Unter den Linden*. It was usually bustling with people, automobiles and horse carts—carts were frequently used due to the restraint on fuel—, but that wintery afternoon the street seemed dull and dismal with its stark lime trees lining the sidewalks, its cold granite buildings reflecting the clouds, and its sluggish pedestrians wrapped in dark coats with felt hats pulled low over their pale faces. Although I was a youngster in this world of adults, I felt surrounded by an ominous fear. I looked at the friendly little horse in Joey's stroller. I could imagine it prancing and neighing in a meadow full of daisies where air raids and bombs did not exist.

Once we were half way down the boulevard, I tugged at Auntie's coat and begged, "Can I pull the horsey, please!"

I must have been a pest for after a while she stopped the stroller and handed me the toy, which my brother relinquished indifferently.

First I stroked its soft mane and wound its silken tail around my hand. Then I set it on the cobblestone sidewalk and pulled it by its string. But the little wooden horse kept tipping over. I had to stop continuously to set it straight.

"We'll never get to the park!" complained Auntie, who had a fixed schedule in mind. She wanted to be home in time to help Mom prepare our supper.

She scooped up the little horse and put it in her leather bag. I cried and stamped my feet. She was a stern old maid with no authority in our household.

"I want to hold the little horse," I screamed. "Give it to me! Give it to me!"

I was rather spoiled with my mom constantly fussing over my fine blond hair and decking me out in frilly dresses. I knew my impertinence would win. People stopped and stared. Auntie was embarrassed and gave me back the toy.

"You must be careful," she warned. "You must not pull it over those stones. Carry it till we get to the park. There, you and Joey can pull it on the smooth paths."

I smiled happily and clutched my treasure to my heart. Red banners with swastikas were floating from the upper windows of buildings and decorating the Brandenburg Gate, but I did not ask questions. At home I had learned not to talk about certain things. Therefore I did not point at the flags. Something else caught my eye. A group of men, women and children in black coats and shawls were gathered on the corner of the sidewalk ahead of us. Soldiers with long grey coats and guns strapped over their shoulders walked about and made a dull sound with their tall leather boots. I could not see the cause of the commotion, but I glimpsed a horse lying on its flank, a real horse harnessed to a cart. The cart was turned over and the horse was whinnying and rearing its head with terrified eyes.

"What is the matter with the horse?" I asked Auntie.

"Don't look, Erika," she said in a hoarse whisper. "These people are Jews. The SS are taking them away!"

"Can we look at the horse?" I cried unmindful of the crowd. Auntie grabbed my hand and gave it a mighty jolt.

"Don't look!" she repeated under her breath and pushed the stroller past the silent group. Sensing her anxiety, I held on to her like on the black-out nights when we rushed to the bunkers.

After we had crossed the street, she let go of my hand and relaxed her pace.

"Where is Joey's horse?" she asked. I looked at my empty hands.

"You dropped it!" she cried. We both looked behind us. A small white and red object lay on the curb near the mass of people.

"We can't go back," she said and pursed her lips, not so much in sorrow for having lost the toy as in dismay at the scene before us.

An army truck had parked. Soldiers in long grey coats jumped out and marshaled the crowd into the truck's open back.

"They take them away even if they are converted Catholics," muttered Auntie. "They've gone into convents and monasteries and hauled out nuns and priests! God will punish them!"

Her eyes were hard and bitter. She was a devout Bavarian who recited her rosary every night. If God turned against *them*, she predicted no good. *They* would be left in the devil's hands.

I never questioned who *they* were for *they* were the mighty ones, the terrible ones with important ribbons and medals, who were mentioned in fearful whispers and whose names I must never repeat for *they* had the power to take my father away, and even the rest of us, to a dark place worse than a prison.

I saw a soldier walk up to our little horse and stare at it. He bent down slowly and picked up the toy. He turned it over in his large gloved hands and looked about for its owner, but, finding none, he walked to the army truck. Meanwhile, the city workers were straightening the upturned cart and leading away the ailing horse.

Before Auntie could rush us to the park, I quickly turned my head. I saw that our little horse had changed hands. A dark haired girl standing at the rear of the army truck was clasping it in her arms. She looked at me with large sad eyes and smiled. Perhaps she had seen me drop the toy.

Auntie told me that these trucks were carrying people to places of horror. One wrong word or move could send us to that place as well. Later I found out that my father was secretly listening to the clandestine BBC radio station and giving medical help to "certain patients" hidden in basements.

When we returned to our apartment, Auntie explained the situation to my mother. The pretty little horse was never mentioned again. But sometimes at night I saw it in my dreams. It was a beautiful white stallion galloping in fields of daisies. The little dark haired girl and I were riding it joyfully, far away from the grey city of war and sadness.

Deep in thought, I left the Brandenburg Gate and strolled past the massive government edifices rebuilt after the war. Everything was new and polished, yet heavy with memories. I stopped at a café in the

*Lustgarten* near the Spree and watched the young people of the rally come down the boulevard. They were linking arms and singing as they headed towards the clubs and entertainment venues of this vibrant city.

How things have changed! I entered a souvenir shop on the *Kurfuerstendam* and bought a small replica of the Brandenburg Gate to take home with me and remind me in Canada that I too was once a *Berlinerin*.

*"If we have no peace, it is because we have forgotten that we belong to each other."*

*Mother Teresa*

# Onions

**A** trivial incident of childhood takes me back to those terrible Berlin days. Like many little ones I was a fussy eater when it came to healthy foods like soups, vegetables and salads. My father's unmarried sisters, Auntie Marie and Auntie Rete, were living with us in our large apartment and helping my pregnant Mom with Joey and me in the evenings. During the day, they assisted Dad in his busy medical practice on the floor below ours.

Auntie Marie and Auntie Rete were often frustrated with my reluctance for what they considered wholesome foods. They would coax, bribe and even threaten me. They would pull out an illustrated book by Wilhelm Busch and point at a fat little boy, named Kasper, who refused to eat his soup and grew skinnier day after day until he was a mere skeleton. They pointed at his grave topped by a cross as a warning, but I was not impressed and stubbornly refused my meals.

Onions are now one of my favourite condiments, but when I was a little girl, I hated them with a passion. Even after my mother and my aunts had assured me that they had removed all onions from my portions, I would discover their obnoxious transparent slivers and push my plate aside.

It was my mother's birthday. Auntie Marie and her younger sister, Auntie Rete, had taken the day off from Dad's busy office to prepare a sumptuous feast with all kinds of Bavarian recipes from their native region. They had been chopping and cooking all day, and in the evening they explained to little Joey and me that we would be sitting in the dining room with the big people, and that we would have to behave and eat everything on our plate like good little children.

They helped me into my blue velvet dress and dressed my little brother in his new checkered suit. They propped us on pillows in the upholstered chairs of our elegant dining room. Auntie Marie sat down beside Joey and Auntie Rete near me. My dad, the doctor, took the head of the table and surveyed us briefly through his steel rimmed glasses. He always looked worried and tired these days. My beautiful mom looked lovely in her flowery silken gown and her blond hair pinned back in an artful chignon. She wore the pearl necklace Dad had given her. She sat down demurely by his side and smiled at us.

Our dinner table looked enchanting under our crystal chandelier. Everything sparkled: the Rosenthal plates, the silver cutlery, and the porcelain tureens filled with steaming ragouts. A centerpiece of white roses added to the festive air. I peeked at a chocolate *Kirschtorte* topped with whipped cream, waiting on a counter for our dessert.

My hands on the table and my elbows tucked in like a little lady, I watched the adults chat pleasantly and help themselves to the delicious dishes and Rhineland wines. But someone, or perhaps the collective will of my aunts and dear Mom, who was much younger and more naive than my aunts, had decided that for my cultural benefit I should sample all the foods on the table.

I stared with horror at the appetizer someone had slipped on my plate: tomato slices sprinkled with onions that clung to them like minute worms! Real worms could not have repulsed me more. I knew I could not escape my ordeal.

With a big sigh I speared a tomato slice on my fork. If only I could remove the obnoxious onions! I would have liked to use my fingers, but my aunts, who were watching me like hawks, would not permit such incivility. In silent agony, I gazed at the adults babbling and laughing, and at my little brother Joey smearing up his cheeks with sauces.

"Why don't you eat your fine vegetables?" asked Auntie Rete, my younger and gentler aunt. "It is your Mommy's birthday. She'd be so happy if you did."

"The onions!" I whispered.

"The onions are tiny. Besides, onions are good for little girls," she insisted.

"I don't like them," I murmured, afraid that her older sister would hear me. I knew that Auntie Marie would call me a bad girl and reproach Mom for raising me without discipline. It was so difficult to guess what grown-ups expected me to do! Unless I was quiet and invisible, I was sure to offend them. I looked at Mom in hopes that she would rescue me, but she was amusing Dad with her stories.

"Eat your salad or you won't have any birthday cake," said Auntie Rete. "It's your favorite *Torte*!"

I took a deep breath and closed my eyes. I imagined guiding the obnoxious tomato into my mouth, chewing it quickly and gulping it down, onions and all. But when I opened my eyes, it still hung on my fork, its onion bits glistening under the crystal lights.

"The child is not eating. That's why she's so skinny," cried Auntie Marie who had observed my antics. I cringed. In a moment she would tell Mom that I was bad.

"Eat!" Auntie Rete encouraged me. "Think of all the poor children in Africa who have no food!"

I could neither imagine these children nor their connection with my salad. Africa seemed as far away as a planet. It had blue skies, golden sunshine and green grass like in the Bible stories Mom read to me at night. It had beautiful princesses who bathed in a big river. In Africa there were no air raids that made you rush in panic through the streets, no noisy planes that dropped bombs at night.

"Remember the Torte!" said Auntie Rete with an encouraging smile.

Auntie Marie looked at me with disgust and turned to Mom. "The child should be spanked. It's terrible to let her be stubborn like that!"

Mom, intimidated by the older woman, blushed and said sweetly. "Won't you try, Erika? Think of it as a birthday present for me!"

I adored Mom and would have given her all the treasures in the world. Eating onions did not seem a gift. I could not do it.

"Erika deserves a good beating!" declared the sanguine aunt. She faced Dad, "The child doesn't eat! It will stunt her growth!"

Dad looked alarmed. He was much older than Mom and carried a constant frown, even when Mom was telling him stories about the silly things we did. He was a conscientious man. "Not eating will harm her health," he observed with medical concern.

"A good spanking will make her eat," insisted the older aunt. Dad flushed with anger. I knew I was disgracing him in front of his sisters. Mom tried to hold him back with soothing words, but he pushed her aside. He strode towards me, his forehead creased in an deep frown, his icy blue eyes behind his steel rimmed glasses fixed on mine. I froze in my chair.

"Are you going to eat, Erika?"

I looked miserably at my tomato salad, unable to see it clearly through my tears. His strong hands lifted me out of my chair. "I will make you eat!" he scowled. Just then the air raid alarm howled like a giant beast trying to enter our dining room through its satin curtains. In its high pitched whine we could hear the thundering roar of planes, so close by that it seemed they were about to crash through our roof.

Mom and my aunts left the table with hysterical cries, "Schnell! Schnell! Hurry! Hurry!" They rushed to the corners of the room where their valuables were tied up in bundles.

Joey dropped his spoon and started to shriek, like he always did when the sirens wailed.

Dad looked at me with an ashen face. "Come, Erika," he said as calmly as he could. "We must run quickly. They sounded the alarm too late. We must head for the shelters."

All the lights went out. Someone helped me into my coat. We hurried down the dark stairs of our apartment building and ran through the deafening noise and blacked out streets with the horde of panicked people rushing to the shelters.

I felt Mom's hand clasp me tightly as she ran beside my terrified aunts and my dad carrying my screaming little brother. I felt reassured with my parents and aunts beside me, in spite of the terrible roar of planes and the firebombs falling like bright candles and raining sparks all around us.

We did not finish our birthday meal or eat our delicious *Kirschtorte*, for that night (or was it some other night?) our apartment building, like the other buildings in our district, was razed to the ground. I was told little about this, as my parents did not want to traumatize us, their little ones, with the terrible news.

We moved to a small property Dad had bought in the suburbs, in a village called Braunsdorf near the Oder-Spree canal. My mother, the children (my mother gave birth to twins) and my father's aunt, whom we called *Tante* (Auntie), stayed there in a small cottage.

My father, with his sisters Rete and Marie, remained in Berlin where he resumed his stressful medical practice in a new building.

With our departure from Berlin, we left behind our city life amidst torn up streets and ravaged buildings. My mother and Auntie got busy settling us into our new country life. They cooked hearty potatoes, broths and puddings on the cast iron stove of our country kitchen and fixed up cozy little beds for Joey and me. While my mother nursed the twins, a lengthy process, Joey and I were free to roam through the meadows and fields behind our house, gather flowers, and collect insects and snails. My father came sometimes from the city to relax with us. He set up an apiary near the garden. I remember his white outfit that protected him from head to toe from the bees and the sweet taste of honeycombs he brought into the house.

In addition to the twins, Helga and Ute, another little girl, Burgi (Margie), completed our busy household before we fled to Austria at the end of the war.

*"I know not with what weapons World War III will be fought,*
*but World War IV will be fought with sticks and stones."*

*Albert Einstein*

# The Bunker

After our apartment in Berlin had been burned to the ground by an incendiary bomb, my mother and the children moved to our summer house in Braunsdorf, a farming village east of Berlin. Auntie, Dad's Bavarian aunt, who had been his nanny and now was ours, came with us.

In Braunsdorf we lived an almost idyllic life after our former harrowing existence. Our white-washed bungalow with its small kitchen, cozy bedrooms and open porch was simple but comfortable. Behind the house were a shed, a vegetable garden, and to my delight, a large meadow full of wild flowers. I would string garlands of dandelions, daisies and buttercups and stroll about in these delicate ornaments like an imaginary princess.

Large grey planes roared overhead, sometimes so low that our windows rattled, but they wore the familiar swastikas and were of no threat to us. Enemy bombers were not interested in our village; they flew in formation high over us, heading towards Berlin and other important cities they wished to destroy.

Dad continued his medical practice in war torn Berlin. Since he was providing a necessary service to our country, he was not required to join the army. When he visited us by taking a taxi (he had not learned how to drive), he looked exhausted. His face was ashen and drawn, his eyes cold and restless.

One sunny afternoon, while I was standing in the front yard, I was surprised to see my dad in a cheerful mood as he stepped out of his taxi. I watched him run sprightly up the steps of our porch and burst into the kitchen where Mom and Auntie were tending to my newborn twin sisters. Then he rushed back out, posted himself in front of our gate, and looked up the road as if he was expecting someone.

Shortly thereafter, a colossal truck drove up with a chunk of cement protruding from its back. Dad waved the truck into our backyard near our shed. Two hefty men jumped out of the cab, opened the back of the truck, and rolled out a huge cement cone. Guided by my dad's booming Bavarian voice, they set it upright in our yard.

I was highly intrigued and walked around the mysterious cone that looked like an ogre's pointed hat dropped from the sky. I watched Dad run his hands over its smooth wall, pull a handle that opened it, and, to my horror, creep into the black belly of the monster, and shut the door behind him. After a few seconds he crawled back out. He nodded with approval and waved the truck drivers away.

"What is it?" I asked. Dad was an important doctor. He did not waste time talking to little girls, not even pastoral princesses decked out in flowers. He observed me through his steel rimmed glasses and said solemnly, "It's a *Bunker*, Erika. A shelter when the bombs fall."

I knew about *Bunkers* that were as big as hotels. In Berlin we used to run to them at night when the terrible sirens howled. But here, there were no air raids, and this structure seemed too small for a shelter. I was puzzled.

"Don't you go near it, Erika," my father warned. "It's not a playhouse."

I quickly returned to my dolls on the porch. I had no desire to go near the ugly monster. Through the open kitchen door I could overhear Mom and Auntie converse in animated voices. They did not trust this atrocity. They even laughed at its small size. My mother would have preferred to ignore it altogether, but she respected my dad's whims.

Dad was extremely proud of his *Bunker*. He walked around it, examined it, and tested its surface with nods of satisfaction. I heard him explain to the women that it was designed to bounce off bombs

24

when they fell from the sky. That is how I understood its function in my childish mind.

Although we were relatively safe in our village of Braunsdorf, Dad said that bombs could accidentally drop from enemy planes heading for Berlin; therefore, our little *Bunker* was essential for our safety.

Dad came often from Berlin to visit us, but on each occasion the war planes showed no desire to loosen their cargo on our village. He looked at his little *Bunker* and grew impatient. He paced nervously the kitchen floor and declaimed loudly. I did not understand his speeches, but watched his hands slice the air. Mom and Auntie were quiet and tense when he expounded his views with terrible names like Hitler, Stalin, Mussolini. "Gangsters! Crooks! Bandits!" he called them, Germans and enemies alike. I trembled with fear and hid in a corner behind a kitchen chair so as to be invisible.

One night, Auntie shook me awake and whispered the terrible words as effective as an alarm, "*Schnell! Schnell!* Hurry! Hurry!"

"There are no sirens!" I objected.

"Be quiet," she hissed through her gums without dentures. She shoved me into my coat and shoes and marshaled me into the kitchen. In the glow of a lantern on the table, I glimpsed Mom in her blue housecoat with my baby twin sisters in her arms, and my little brother Joey clinging to her side, and Auntie in her white nightgown, grey sweater, and straggly braids, hovering about like a restless spirit. Dad, fully dressed, picked up the petroleum lantern whose glow shone on his flushed face and reflected like tiny moons in his steel rimmed glasses.

"*Schnell!*" he cried. "Follow me! We must all go to the *Bunker*."

"But I hear no planes," I said to Auntie.

"Be quiet and do as your father says," she commanded.

We ran out into the cold starry night. Dad was in the lead with his lantern, followed by Mom with the babies and Auntie with little Joey who was wailing. But no one held my hand, for I was a mature four-year- old; I knew how to take care of myself.

The adults crouched to enter the shelter, but the door was high enough for me. We all sat down and squeezed against the cold cement wall. Through the open door of the shelter I glimpsed the gable of our house silhouetted against the glittering stars. Dad shut the door with a clang.

He lifted the lantern and took a count: three adults and four children. He looked at his watch. "Now, we must wait," he said and turned off his lantern. Mom and Auntie whispered excitedly. I listened for the dreadful planes but heard none.

There were strange noises in my head, a fearful pounding. I put my hands over my ears and squeezed my eyes. But the roar in my ears and the red flashes behind my eyelids would not stop. Soon fire would drop through the top of the *Bunker* and blow us apart, bits of heads, arms, legs, all mixed into a human stew, children and adults alike, buried alive in this cone of cement. I wanted to scream but could not utter a sound. The wail of my little brother seemed to be my own. Any minute now we would die. I was sure of it.

I don't know how long I remained immersed in my terror. A whiff of cool air blew across my face. I opened my eyes and saw Auntie's dark shadow in front of the bunker's door.

"What's the matter with you?" she chided and pulled me out with a firm hand. "Everyone's in the house. Come along! Why aren't you moving?"

I looked around like in a trance. All was quiet. There were no fires and no planes. The sky was speckled with trembling stars; the soft glow of the kitchen windows fell in long stripes across the yard.

When we entered the house, I saw Mom with the twin babies in her arms and Joey by her side. Auntie said to her, "Erika fell asleep in the *Bunker*! Imagine spending the night there!"

Dad was standing near the dinner table, his hands covered with blood.

"I cut my hands in the heavy hinges of the *Bunker*," he announced. "Quickly, get iodine and bandages. I don't want to catch an infection."

Mom hurried to the bedroom to put the babies into their cribs and returned with meters and meters of gauze to help Auntie wrap up Dad's hands, his precious doctor's hands, which helped to save lives and wanted so badly to save us in this terrible war.

No one noticed me as I crawled into my corner behind a kitchen chair. My knees tucked in, I cradled my head in my arms and tried to make sense of the frightful images in my head.

After Dad's hands were bandaged and Joey was asleep, Mom found me behind the chair and took me in her arms.

"Why are you hiding, Erika?" she asked.

"I was scared. I was very scared, Mommy."

"I'm so sorry, sweetheart." She stroked my head and explained, "It was a drill. We had to do this in case of real danger."

She tucked me in my duvet bed and sat down by my side. She sang my favorite lullaby very softly so as not to wake up Joey who was asleep in the bed next to mine.

*"Weisst du wieviel Sterlein stehen..."*

*Do you know how many stars are in the heavens?*

*God the Father counted them all, so not a single one will go missing...*

Children were like birds, fish and stars, she said. There were millions of them, but God knew them all and counted them every day because he did not want to lose a single one. Comforted, I fell asleep with the vision of myriads of happy stars whirling under God's watchful eyes.

I visited Braunsdorf in the early 1990's, after our eastern property had been returned to us. Someone had rolled the *Bunker* down to the edge of the Oder-Spree Canal and removed its cement door. I smiled at the grotesque cone, so much smaller than I remembered it. Stranded among wild flowers and weeds, it looked like a play house for children, its grim purpose quite forgotten.

*"War is not an adventure. It is a disease like typhus."*
*Antoine de Saint-Exupery*

# Flowers

Our life was relatively calm and normal in our country house of Braunsdorf in the suburbs of Berlin.—I say 'relatively' because the worry and anxiety instilled by the big war never left us. In this peaceful setting, Mom and Auntie Voit (my father's aunt who had joined our household) had decided to plant several rows of flowers in the vegetable patch behind our house. Most of the flowers were meant for the beehive, a hobby my father pursued as a relaxation from his stressful medical practice in Berlin. The others were grown for the pure enjoyment of their lush beauty.

I was permitted to pick dandelions, daisies and buttercups in our meadow for my princess crowns and necklaces, but I was not allowed to touch the flowers of the garden. Sometimes, when I thought no one was looking, I would climb up the garden's picket fence to admire and smell the bright beauties that had opened overnight: fluffy dahlias, slim jonquils, and delicate roses that swayed in the breeze. But if I as much as reached out to feel their petals, Auntie, who watered them twice a day and watched them like a hawk, would lean out of the kitchen window and shriek, "Erika, you naughty girl, get away from my flowers!"

These treasures were reserved for special occasions like birthdays, celebrations and the visit of Opa and Oma, my grandparents from Oberschefflenz, and other relatives.

One morning, when I went out to play in the meadow as usual, I was surprised to find my beautiful mom in the midst of these gorgeous flowers. Mom hardly ever visited the garden. She spent most of her time in the bedroom where she nursed my newborn twin sisters, Helga and Ute. The garden was Auntie's domain. But that morning Mom strolled through the garden in her blue silken dress whose frills wafted gently in the breeze. She was wearing a brimmed hat with a velvet ribbon. I watched her snip flowers here and there and gather them into a lovely bouquet. Intrigued, I sneaked into the garden and approached her. I knew she would not shoo me away like Auntie, for she was gentle and soft spoken and did not uphold rules, although she allowed Dad and Auntie to dictate laws for us. Something sad and thoughtful in her demeanor made me hesitate before I pulled lightly on her dress.

"Why do you pick flowers, Mommy?"

She looked at me with her blue eyes full of tears.

"Why are you crying?" I asked perturbed. "Is it Daddy? Did he get hurt?

Dad was working in Berlin and always brought dreadful news about the bombings in the city.

"No, no. Daddy's fine," she said quickly and brushed away her tears.

"Did somebody die?"

Two family members had died recently: Dad's father in Landshut, because he could not get medications for his pneumonia, and Dad's little brother Hans, an engineering student, who had disappeared in a reconnaissance mission over the Mediterranean. Everyone had been very sad.

Mom hesitated before she answered. "No one died," she said, but her eyes were moist.

"What's the matter, Mommy?"

She tried to smile and held out her flowers. I smelled with delight the fluffy red dahlias and the white rosebuds dotting her bouquet.

"We are having a party?" I asked brightly.

"No, no party."

I was little, but I knew something was wrong. I walked with her in silence along the flower beds.

After a while I asked, "Who are these flowers for?"

"For someone in the hospital in Berlin. I'm going to Berlin this afternoon."

"Will Daddy be there?"

"Yes, and Oma and Opa too. Auntie Ulla is driving me."

Ulla was Mom's little sister. She was a medical student in Berlin. She cut her blond hair in a bob, a style Auntie called *Bubikopf* with a sneer. She wore smart outfits and held her head high. Auntie, who had grown up on a Bavarian farm, did not care for her fancy airs.

"Can I come along?"

"No, darling. You will stay here with Auntie. She will make supper for you and Joey and tuck you in your beds in the evening."

"But I want to go with you. I'm a big girl. I will be very good."

"You'll come some other time," she said and stroked my head. "Do you remember Uncle Henry who went to war?"

I nodded. Henry was Mom's little brother. He was a tall curly-haired boy who laughed a lot and made jokes. He used to throw me up in the air and swing me around till I was dizzy.

"Yes I remember him."

"Well, he is in the hospital. Children are not allowed to see him."

Auntie came running toward us. She frowned a little when she saw me in the garden, but said nothing.

"Hurry!" she cried to Mom. "Your sister is here. She is waiting for you in the car."

"Just give me a minute!" said Mom. She quickly smoothed back a blond curl that had escaped from her chignon and tucked it under her sun hat.

"I'll need my coat," she said.

Auntie looked down at me, then asked her sternly, "You did not tell Erika about your brother, did you?"

"No, I didn't," said Mom.

"Children must not know about these things. It'll shock their minds and stunt their development. Children must only hear happy things."

"I know," said Mom. "I did not tell her."

Mom ran into the house to get her summer coat. Auntie followed her.

Auntie Ulla was waiting in the beige Volkswagen Opa had given her when she began her medical studies. She wore her brown feathered hat tilted elegantly over her brow. Her pale blue eyes darted about. Her rouged lips twitched nervously as she sucked on a long cigarette.

"If you don't hurry, Sis," she yelled in the direction of the open kitchen door, "the hospital will be closed to visitors and you won't see him."

"What's the matter with Uncle Henry?" I asked her.

"Doesn't your mother tell you anything?" she snarled.

"No."

"Well, then I'll tell you. You should know because you'll see him when he comes back from the hospital. The Russians shot him in Leningrad. His left arm was amputated, cut off right here at the shoulder." She demonstrated with a wave of her cigarette. "Now he has no arm and he is only twenty! He wanted to be a doctor like his dad. He'll never be a doctor now!"

She laughed bitterly and blew puffs of smoke into the blue sky. "Listen, little Erika, everyone's crying and sad, but I'm laughing. Guess what? He won't have to go back to the front. Ha! Ha! Now he is as useless to *them* as a post. The others will die, but he'll be around when the war is over. He is a lucky fellow! Yes, little Erika, Henry is a lucky man."

I did not like what she said. I frowned and tried to understand why it was lucky to have an arm cut off. I hung my left arm limply by my side and imagined what it would be like to do everything with one hand. I would not be able to make dolls out of acorns and weave necklaces of daisies. No, I would not like losing my arm! Grown-ups were strange people.

I watched Mom climb carefully with her beautiful dahlias and white rosebuds into Auntie Ulla's cabriolet, and I waved her good-bye as she drove off with her sister to Berlin.


I visited my uncle Henry several times during my travels overseas. He was a retired forester living happily with his wife and daughter Gita in Pforzheim. He drove me around Baden to show me the many woods he had tended in the Rhine region. Once in a while he complained about his "phantom arm," but this handicap did not stop him from enjoying the small pleasures of life like hunting, hiking, dancing, and even tennis.

On one of my visits, he showed me a photograph in which he and his young classmates were boarding a military train, suitcases in hand and big smiles on their faces. "Look at us, idiots," he said. "We couldn't wait to go to the front!" Then he turned to me and sighed, "Not one of them made it back, except me."

*"Each one prays to God according to his own light."*
*Mahata Ghandi*

# Where is God?

It is the delight of parents to dress up their children like dolls and have them perform. What parents do not know is that shy little ones become utterly confused when faced with this predicament.

The following Sunday was *Fronleichnam*, the feast of Corpus Cristi in the Catholic church, celebrated with a solemn procession in which a golden vested priest carries the "sacred host" through the streets and blesses the various altars decorated along the way. Devout parishioners, some of them carrying religious flags, follow him with chants and prayers while flower girls strew rose petals in his path.

It was my mom's and my aunts' wonderful idea to make me look as cute as a button so that I could join the little girls in this procession. They talked themselves into such a frenzy of excitement that, in spite of my reluctance, I was forced to participate in this event.

With much trepidation I let my smiling aunts dress me in the frilly white dress my mom had sewn. They adorned my wavy blond hair with a crown of daisies and put white bows on my shoes.

"She looks like an angel!" beamed Auntie Rete, my dad's little sister.

"But she stands stiff like a post," complained Auntie Voit, an older aunt.

"Smile, Erika! No one is going to eat you!" said Auntie Rete.

Mom laughed and tied a little basket adorned with ribbons around my neck.

"Put your hands in it, Erika, to see if it fits. You will be scattering flower petals before God," she said with reverence.

"God?" I asked amazed. "Will I see Him?"

I imagined a bearded old man in a long white robe like in the Bible stories my mother read to me at bedtime. He knew when I was bad and teased and pinched my little brother Joey. I did not want to see God. "I don't want to go to church!" I said.

"But you must. It is Sunday. It is a big sin not to go to church on Sunday!"

I sighed.

"Besides you have a pretty dress," said Auntie Rete. "Your mommy sewed it for you, and she made the trimmings for your basket. You must not disappoint your mom!"

The cathedral in Fuerstenwalde was several kilometers away. My mom and my aunts, dressed in bright summer hats and light coats, were already pulling out their bikes. A neighbor was watching Joey and the twins while we were away. My dad could not come with us. He had to stay at his medical practice in Berlin.

I sat at the back of my younger aunt's bike. I liked Auntie Rete. She was cheerful and listened to me. She was not like Auntie Voit, who hardly ever talked to me except to remind me of proper behavior.

I looked down from the back seat of Auntie Rete's bike and watched pebbles on the roadside swim by like grey eels. I glanced out at the green fields, so peaceful and beautiful with early buttercups and daisies. I looked up at the blue sky, so lovely with cottony clouds where the angels lived when the war planes did not chase them away. May be meeting God was not so terrible after all. I never understood why He lived in the ugly dark cathedral of Fuerstenwalde. It must be lonely and depressing to stay in the midst of stone pillars and cold statues. No wonder He was such an unfriendly God.

When we dismounted in front of the massive gothic church, I was assailed by my mom's and my aunts' fretting. They smoothed down my hair, fluffed the frills of my dress, and adjusted my crown of flowers. Like always when I was nervous, I had to go to the bathroom. This caused a disturbance and delayed their plans.

When I returned, we entered the crowded cathedral. The church looked dark and forbidding after the bright sunshine outside. The organ peal reverberated through my body and filled me with apprehension. A heavy scent of incense permeated the air. We found a spot at the back, away from two officers in uniform. (Mom had told me that they made sure that the priest would not preach against the government.)

The Eucharistic procession had already begun. The priest and his train of parishioners were walking slowly and reverently along the aisles and pausing for songs and prayers at the various altars of the saints. Because of the danger of air raids, the religious ceremony took place indoors instead of outdoors as was custom.

My aunts hung my pretty basket around my neck and filled it with the flower petals Mom had brought in a brown paper bag. I stood mute and bewildered like a porcelain doll. Instructions were pouring in from all sides, but I understood none of them.

"Here comes the priest, darling. You go in the procession with the little girls dressed in white and scatter your rose petals before God!" said Auntie Rete.

"Where is God?" I asked and looked around.

"Here He is!" whispered Mom and pointed at the priest holding up a gigantic monstrance sparkling with gold and jewels. Beside him, altar boys in white robes and red cassocks were swinging silver crucibles of incense. But I could not see God.

Mom and my aunts pushed me gently into the procession of flower girls, who were walking ahead of the priest, and whispered in my ear, "Go with them and do as they do!"

I followed the young girls in white dresses and flower crowns. They were taller than I, and I felt lost and bewildered among them. My basket was pulling at my neck. I picked carefully one petal and dropped it on the ground. I remembered that I was not to scatter them all at once. After a few steps I dropped another petal, then another one, while solemn hymns echoed in my ears.

I walked diligently down the alleys, following the flower girls and pausing at the side altars when they did, until I returned to the spot where Mom and my two aunts were waiting. They rushed at me, poked at my basket and spoke in low voices so as not to disturb the worshippers.

"You still have your flowers!  You were supposed to throw them!"

"But I did throw the petals!"

"No, you did not!  They are still in your basket!"

"She is a dumb one!" said Auntie Voit with a sneer.  Mom was embarrassed and blushed.

"She'll know next time," said Auntie Rete to excuse me.

But I knew I had disappointed them.  I hung my head and followed the rest of the mass, dwarfed in a forest of singing adults, who stood up and knelt in turn.

After the ceremony we followed the crowd of parishioners out of the cathedral and down the steps. Mom and my aunts returned to their bikes.

"Hop on," said Auntie Rete.

"Can I keep my basket?" I asked.

"Of course," she said.

I straddled the back of her bike.  "God is in the sky," she said when we were on the road again.  "You can scatter your flowers now."

I looked at the balmy sky filled with angel clouds scudding in the wind.  I dug my little hands into my basket and threw handfuls of flower petals into the air.  I watched them flutter pink, blue and yellow like butterflies over the meadows and fields, a fitting homage to God, a joyful God full of sunshine, not the grey sad one trapped in the cold dark church of Fuerstenwalde where no one could see Him.

When I arrived home, my basket was empty, and I was happy that no one commented on my performance.  More pressing matters filled everyone's mind.  Dad had heard rumors, confirmed by the clandestine radio station he listened to secretly, that the Germans were losing the war and that Russian troops were advancing towards us. He started making plans for our safety.

*"War is only a cowardly escape from the problems of peace."*
                                                    *Thomas Mann*
*"An eye for an eye only ends up making the whole world blind."*
                                                    *Mahatma Ghandi*

# Doll Village

In spite of this terrible time of war and devastation, we children enjoyed a relatively carefree existence on our property in Braunsdorf, away from the bombardments in Berlin. Mom and Auntie Voit drowned their anxiety in the numerous domestic tasks associated with raising four small children. Mom nursed my twin sisters, Helga and Ute, and weighed each infant after her milk intake to make sure that she had been nourished sufficiently. Auntie, my father's aunt, took on the heavier domestic chores; she chopped wood, gardened, cooked, cleaned the house, and kept a watchful eye on my little brother Joey and me.

On Sundays, the day of the Lord, Auntie usually put her chores aside and hiked with Joey and me outside of the village to give Mom a rest. On that particular Sunday of spring, however, Mom announced that she would take us for a walk.

"I have a surprise for you," she said. "Put on your coats quickly and we will go for a walk in the big black forest."

"What surprise?" I asked.

"You'll see," she said and smiled.

"Will you tell us stories?"

"Of course!"

Mom knew the best fairy tales in the world and loved to tell them with drama and suspense. Auntie did not want to come along and took the opportunity to attend an afternoon service in the church. Auntie prayed a lot with her rosary for her dead mother, her brothers who had died in the first big war, and her nephews who were in the army now.

Mom wrapped my twin infant sisters in embroidered blankets and tucked them into their elegant twin wicker carriage. She put on her fur coat, felt hat and kid gloves. We were comfortable in those days. Dad was a busy practitioner in Berlin.

We set out on a soft country road that cut through green meadows and cultivated fields. Joey looked for beetles and snails, and I picked cornflowers and poppies that grew abundantly on the edge of fields. A sudden gust of wind shook the trees and blew dust in our faces. We looked up at the sky that had been blue just a while ago. Large black clouds were scudding across the horizon and blocking out the sun. Mom frowned.

"What's wrong, Mom?" I asked.

She explained that if the dark clouds looked like men on horseback, evil soldiers were on their way. I had heard Mom and Auntie whisper that the Russian men would do horrible things if they came to our village. Mom sighed with relief. "Thank God, Erika, there are no horse riders in the clouds. We are safe for now."

As we were looking up, the dark clouds swirled apart and sunlight flooded through them like a golden waterfall.

"What is it?" I cried.

"It's God's eye," said my mom who liked to keep us in wonder.

"Can He see us?" I asked.

"Of course. God sees everything."

I thought about this for a while and remembered the terrible ruins and fires in Berlin where we used to live and where Dad was working still. He was always stressed and upset and full of bad news when he visited us.

"Why doesn't God stop the bad planes that drop the bombs?" I asked.

Mom sighed. "Some people are bad. That is why God lets bad things happen."

"I wish God would make the bombs go away so Daddy would be safe."

Mom didn't answer. She looked very sad like when she talked about friends who had died. I gave her my bouquet of poppies and cornflowers. She took them and smiled.

"Go play, Erika," she said.

I watched Joey trot and kick up dust like a horse and whack weeds with a short branch. I was not interested in his games.

"Tell me about princesses," I said and pestered her with questions. How could the princess feel a pea through the mattresses? How did the princess's kiss change the frog into a prince? Why did Rumpelstitskin want the queen's baby? Mom had answers for everything.

We left our path through the fields and meadows and entered a gloomy forest. Tall dark forbidding pine trees surrounded us like in the story of Hansel and Gretel. There was no sound except the shuffle of our feet and the squeak of the baby carriage. The twins were fast asleep. Joe, sensing my fear, threw away his stick and hung on to Mom's coat.

"Are there witches?" I whispered.

A horrible thought occurred to me. Perhaps Mom wanted to lose us like in the story of Hansel and Gretel. She had so many children and Auntie said that the stork would bring us another one!

"Of course, there are witches with long crooked noses and red eyes," said Mom quite seriously. "But they won't catch you if you stay close to me." She looked around, searching the bushes and trees with her eyes. "It must be here. Someone told me it was here."

We came to a clearing on a grassy knoll. "Look, Erika! Look, Joey!" she cried. "Here is the surprise!"

Joey and I ran up the knoll where she pointed and shrieked with delight. A miniature doll village, a sort of Disneyland, was tucked among the grasses, mosses and rocks, rows and rows of painted wooden houses, schools, hospitals and churches. I crouched in the grass to examine their daintily carved windows, doors and balconies, and their exquisite little tables, chairs and beds. Soldiers on leave or convalescing had built this doll village before leaving for the front. But there were no little people in them.

"Where are the dolls?" I asked.

"They ran away," said Mom.

"Because of the war?"

"May be. Perhaps they are hiding in the forest," she said.

I looked at the deserted doll village. Poor little dolls having to hide in the black forest under roots of trees and behind shrubs where it is dark and damp!

"Mom, if bad soldiers come, are we going to hide there?"

Mom glanced at the deep forest with its dense undergrowth almost as black as a witch's oven in the falling light. She shuddered and her eyes grew wide with fear. "Don't say silly things, Erika!" she said in a trembling voice. "It's getting dark. Auntie is waiting for us for supper!"

We returned along the gloomy forest path with the tall pines on either side looming over us like ogres with many arms. Joey and I held on to the baby carriage. The twins woke up and wailed but Mom did not stop to nurse them. She hurried us along until we were back on the open road.

"And the soldiers?" I asked. "Where are the soldiers who built the doll houses?"

"In the war," she said.

"Are they going to die?"

"May be," she sighed.

"Then they won't see their doll village again."

"Some will come back if we say our prayers," she added quickly.

"That will be wonderful! The little dolls will come back and live in their doll houses!"

I clapped my hands and skipped happily. The black clouds had disappeared and pink and golden streaks glimmered in the west. May be God was not angry with the bad people anymore and all would be well like in the fairy tales.

This was not to be. My dad was recruited with all able men and boys in the last months of the war.

In the spring of 1945, Russian troops advanced into Braunsdorf on their way to Berlin. The panicked villagers, mostly women and children, hid in the forest where we had walked. Some died and disappeared. Others returned to their homes in the village.

Before leaving for the front, Dad had arranged our escape to Austria where Mom, Auntie and his little children (we were five then) would be safe until his return.

*"If you want your children to be intelligent, read them fairy tales…"*
*Albert Einstein*
*"I saw an angel in the marble and carved until I set him free."*
*Michelangelo*

# Potato Heads

Mom was only twenty years old when she married Dad who was fifteen years her senior. She always loved and respected him, even in his most difficult moments. Although she never revealed to us why she had so many children during the war, I am quite sure that Dad took it as a sign of his virility, as to Mom —she simply loved having babies: the pregnancy, the cuddling, and the breast feeding of the little ones. Auntie Voit, my father's aunt, did the heavier chores like washing diapers, scrubbing floors, and taking care of our needs, while Mom rested her swollen belly, nursed her babies, and helped Auntie with the meals. Dad, busy with his medical practice in Berlin, did not interfere in women's affairs.

Mom had grown up in the romantic Rhine region near Heidelberg, a region filled with medieval history and legends. I still can see her sitting by our bedside and carrying us with her gentle voice into the magical world of Grimm's fairy tales, Germanic legends, and Bible stories. I remember gazing at a picture of baby Moses adrift on the Nile and pestering her with questions, or gasping with horror at the witch who had lured Hansel and Gretel into her gingerbread house. Sometimes, Mom was so weary that her voice waned and her eyes fell shut, but I did not let her rest and corrected her speedily if she left out a single detail.

During the daytime she helped Auntie in the kitchen or embroidered little smocks for us. She liked to dress us up and put ribbons in our hair. She never disciplined us -- that was Auntie's job-- but she did reproach us mildly if we did a faux-pas like using our knife to cut potatoes, a no-no at a German table. Most of the time she let us run around wildly with no other restraint than Auntie's continuous scolding. As the young wife of an older man, she left decision-making to her husband and household management to his more experienced aunt, our Auntie.

When I think of her in those days, I think of a child playing with dolls, the last one always her favorite. The rest of us, without being neglected, were left to Auntie, who dressed, combed, fed and supervised us. Sometimes we were allowed into Mom's room to watch the new baby's little mouth disappear in her large blue veined breast. We could touch the baby's little feet, but never its head. We often felt left out, but she was too young and innocent to understand child psychology. She gave us her time by telling us fairy tales and singing lullabies at night.

One of her favorite pastimes in Braunsdorf, where we lived in those days, was to entertain us with puppet shows. Mom did not have wooden puppets, so she created her own. She carved noses, cheeks and mouths into potatoes of various shapes, endowed them with button eyes, woolen hair and beards, and clothed them in colorful scraps of material she wrapped around her fist. A finger inserted in a hole at the bottom of each potato permitted her to bob her puppets on a stage made out of a bed sheet draped over chairs.

Wide-eyed with anticipation, we would sit on pillows before this precarious stage. I, the eldest, would set the tone for my fidgety brother and twin sisters.

A lovely princess with long blond curls and a golden crown would invariably glide across the stage, followed by her father, a severe black bearded king, who insisted that she marry his evil counselor.

Mom would mimic the voices.

"No Father, no!" the princess would squeak.

"Yes, Cunegonde! You must marry him!" the king would growl.

In would trot a handsome prince on a stick horse, a tiny sword in his hands. He would announce heroically, "I will find the Nibelungen treasure! I will kill the terrible dragon and marry the beautiful princess."

The Nibelungen treasure in Germanic folklore was a legendary heap of gold buried in the Rhine River and guarded by a ferocious dragon. Of course, the green dragon with fiery tongue would cross the stage and roar loudly and frighten my little sisters.

Mom was not good at scripts and kept words at a minimum. Most of her effort went into dressing and animating her puppets. But she was as enthusiastic about her plays as we were in watching them.

The red devil in full regalia with pitchfork and horns was our favorite. He would beat up the screaming counselor, drag him to hell, and have us roll over with laughter.

Much to my annoyance, my little siblings would sometimes tumble into the curtain, drag it to the floor and reveal our poor mom on her knees in the midst of a carnage of potato heads with gaping eyes and bloody lips; but our good-natured mom, bursting out in laughter, would gather us in her arms and promise to tell us the whole story at night.

My childish imagination was filled with the marvelous world of Grimm's fairy tales whose heroes never died, whose fire breathing dragons never singed, and whose maidens in distress were always rescued by Prince Charming. This make believe world was more real to me than the grim reality of incendiary bombs, marching soldiers and disturbing politics. Somewhere there was a bright world where evil was conquered, and dragons, witches and ogres defeated. Mom reassured us indirectly through her optimistic attitude that someday war and destruction would end, and peace and harmony would return to our world.

What happened to the potato heads after the play? Of course, Auntie, who never wasted a morsel, made them into her delicious Bavarian *Knoedel* whose secret recipe she never fully revealed to anyone.

## German Potato Dumplings (Knoedel)

*750g potatoes:*
*Boil in water and simmer till soft. Peel and press while hot through a food press.*
*Put them aside till the next day.*

*500 g raw and peeled potatoes.*
*Grate into a bowl with water, then press them dry through a cheese cloth. Mix*
*with the day old potatoes above.*
*Add to the above potato mix 1 egg, 65 g flour and 1 teaspoon salt. Mix and*
*knead well. (Use flour on your hands to prevent sticking).*
*Shape the dough into baseball (or softball) size balls.*
*Put them carefully into boiling salted water. Bring to a boil again and simmer for*
*15 minutes till well cooked. (They may appear grey).*
*Serve with meat and gravy.*
*Auntie added cubed bread crusts, finely chopped herbs, vegetables and possibly*
*sweet spices.*

*"There are only two lasting bequests we can hope to give our children. One of these is roots, the other, wings."*

*Johann Wolfgang Goethe*

# Christmas Cookies

Most of my childhood memories date back to Braunsdorf where Dad had a small summer property near the Oder-Spree Canal. It was a haven of peace and sunshine for my little brother Joey and me. The wild flowers in the meadows, the anthills in the yard, the aroma of the kitchen where Auntie Voit, my father's aunt, and my ever-pregnant mom bustled about, all these things created an aura of contentment, very distinctive from the anxiety ridden life we had experienced in war time Berlin.

I remember the wide open sky of Braunsdorf, filled with puffy clouds that looked like thousands of sheep going to pasture. This was not the grey fearsome sky of Berlin, squeezed between tall granite buildings, where fighter planes brought havoc at night.

Everyone, even little children, was a sky gazer in those days. Were they friendly planes with swastikas who flew east to fight the Russians, or were they enemy planes from Britain, France and America, who would release their deadly cargo on our cities?

We were relatively safe in this farming village of no strategic importance. Nevertheless, we had a small bunker for our protection. Dad, who had his medical office in Berlin, listened secretly to clandestine British broadcasts and was not deceived by Nazi propaganda. He knew Germany was losing the war.

But war or no war, *Kristkindl* was a sacred custom at Christmas time. Mom and Auntie rushed us to bed early during the fall, so they could bake their traditional cookies and *Stollen* in the kitchen. Oh, the delicious smells that precluded the mysterious arrival of *Kristkindl* who would bring us the shimmering *Tannenbaum*, gingerbread cookies and marvelous toys! The suspense was immense for all the preparations were hidden, but obvious, nevertheless, from the secret behavior of adults and our early bedtimes when we were not sleepy at all.

To calm us down, Auntie, who was our nanny, would take us for walks on earth beaten paths along the fallow fields.

Those were lovely evenings! The sunset would daub the clouds in shades of ruby, pink and orange that gave them the appearance of little round ovens burning on the horizon.

"Look at the fires, Auntie!" I cried.

"Fires? Where?" She looked alarmed.

"In the sky!"

"Those are not fires, silly girl. They are red clouds."

"Why are they red?"

Auntie, who knew nothing about the refraction of light since she had attended school only till the age of ten, quickly came up with a story in her Bavarian way.

"The angels are baking Christmas cookies," she said. "They have ovens in the clouds."

I looked up delighted. In my imagination I saw hundreds of little angels busily kneading dough, flattening it with rolling pins, and cutting out millions of cookies in shapes of stars, trees, and crescents. But a horrible thought made me yank at Auntie's coat.

"Auntie, when the planes come at night, will they drop bombs on the angels?"

"Erika, you silly child! Angels are smart. When they hear planes, they quickly pack up and hide. No bomb can ever harm them. *Kristkindl* would never let them come to harm."

I thought about her words carefully and kicked the dust with my leather boots. I had a bright idea.

"Why don't we have wings so we can fly away when the bad planes come?"

"Darling, God did not make us that way. We only get wings when we die. When we die, we can fly wherever we want."

This was too difficult to understand. Mom always cried when she heard about people who had died in the war. I had never seen dead people and was puzzled. I looked at the clouds that were disappearing in a golden shimmer over the low hills. There must be another world far behind the hazy hills.

"Auntie, what is over the hills?"

"Erika, you are driving me crazy with your silly questions! There are more hills behind those hills."

"And over those hills?"

"More hills," she answered.

"Then there is war everywhere in the world?"

"Yes, everywhere."

"And in the stars too?"

"No, everything is quiet in the stars. God lives there."

Quickening her step, she pushed my little brother's stroller with a firm hand. It was getting cool and it was time for supper. I trotted beside her and tried very hard to imagine God's world in the stars.

Before we entered our house I looked up at the evening sky, wondering if the planes would come tonight and drop their bombs on our roof and make us into angels to fly to the stars.

Although adults screened us from the terrors and anxieties they experienced, we sensed the danger and chaos around us. Like in Brahm's lullaby, our life could end any night. Only God decided if we should wake up again. *"Morgen frueh, wenn Gott will, wirst du wieder geweckt."* Tomorrow, God willing, you shall awaken again.

*"Christmas waves a magic wand over this world, and behold, everything is softer and more beautiful."*

*Norman Vincent Peale*

*"Mankind is a great, an immense family...This is proved by what we feel in our hearts at Christmas."*

*Pope John XXIII*

# Christmas Doll

## A Wrinkle in Christmas

Chin in hand, I sat on the steps of our porch in Braunsdorf and watched fluffy snow flakes, fluttering like tiny angels in the air and then settling on our fruit trees, fences and meadows. A delicious aroma of cinnamon, ginger, and cookie dough drifted through the cracks of our kitchen door. Mom and Auntie had sent my little brother and me outside, so they could prepare for *Kristkindl*. *Kristkindl* would come tonight with a Christmas tree, cookies and toys— but only if we were good. This worried me.

I glanced at Joey pushing his colorful wagons across the porch and remembered that I had been quite nasty last summer. Joey was terrified of the bees of Dad's beehive, so I had played a trick on him. Not just once, but several times. I had yelled, "A bee, a bee!" when there were no bees in sight, just for the pleasure of hearing him scream. Mom and Auntie had rushed out of the house, found him unharmed, and had scolded him for being a "sissy." Now I was sorry.

I asked sweetly, "Joey, can I play with you?"

He looked at me with his big blue eyes and nodded.

I went down on my knees, filled his little freight wagons with blocks of wood and helped him guide them through the tunnels. I hoped *Kristkindl* noted my good deed.

After what seemed an eternity, Auntie called us indoors for supper.

I hurried through my plate of creamed spinach, potatoes and eggs, and kept an eye on the patch of sky above the kitchen curtains because when it was dark, *Kristkindl* would come. The mysterious living room had been shut all day. Mom had been rushing in and out, hiding things under her apron and in towels. She said she was preparing the room for *Kristkindl.*

Dad entered the kitchen after our meal. Chuckling like a little boy, he grabbed our hands and bounced around, getting Joey and me all excited and Auntie upset because she was trying to do the dishes and clean the floor.

"Now we must be very quiet," Dad said and took us to the living room door. "Shshsh, *Kinderlein*, listen!" He put his ear against the door and urged us to do the same. We heard rustling, crinkling, furtive sounds. "We must wait for *Kristkindl*'s silver bell! The silver bell rings when *Kristkindl* is finished, then we can go in."

We heard a merry tingling; our eyes opened wide. Dad turned the door knob and ushered us into the darkened room. In the far end, a Christmas tree with burning candles flickered like a night full of stars. On its branches glittered glazed cookies, gilded walnuts, and red apples! At the base was a colorful Nativity scene. But I saw no toys.

I wanted to ask Mommy where *Kristkindl* had put the toys, but she insisted that we sing first. She led us in front of the Baby Jesus in his straw manger with the holy figurines, shepherds and angels bowed before Him, and she asked us to hold hands.

She intoned reverently her favorite carols, "*Stille Nacht,*" "*Ihr Kinderlein, kommet...*","*O Tannenbaum,*" with Dad joining her in a hearty tenor and Auntie in a weak quiver. Joey and I stared wide eyed at the Christmas tree, taking in its marvels.

After the songs Dad turned on the lights, and Mom and Auntie quickly blew out the dripping candles. I tugged at Mom's woolen skirt. "The toys?" I reminded her, a little afraid that *Kristkindl* had forgotten me.

Mom took my hand. "Let's look, Erika, let's look!" she cried and ran with me behind the tree. She pushed a branch aside. I froze as if struck by lightning.

Behind the tree stood a little girl, a real little girl almost as tall as I! She looked at me with sparkling blue eyes and held out her arms with a rosy smile. My heart beat wildly. She wore a red brimmed hat over her shiny black curls, a matching coat and small leather boots.

"You like the present *Kristkindl* brought you, Erika?" asked my mom, but I could neither move nor talk.

Mom blushed with happiness and nudged me. "She's your doll, Erika! Take her."

Mom laid the beautiful doll in my arms. I watched the doll's bright eyes with long lashes fall shut. I lifted her gently. Her blue eyes opened again.

A sudden shriek interrupted my rapture. Auntie had given Joey his gift, a fluffy teddy bear, but Joey had grabbed his teddy and hurled it at the tree whose cookies and apples shook and clanged.

"I don't like the bear," he howled. "I want a doll! I want a doll!"

He dove at me and tried to tear the doll out of my arms. Mom and Auntie held him back in horror.

"Boys don't play with dolls!" cried Auntie.

Mom begged, "Joey, play with your nice teddy bear."

But Joey stamped his feet. "I want a doll! I want a doll!"

Highly alarmed, Mom and Auntie looked at Dad in his leather armchair. Dad got up and cleared his throat. He seemed momentarily confused and turned to the women, "Am I hearing right? Is my son asking for a doll?"

Mom said quickly, "He doesn't like his teddy bear. It is the wrong gift. May be *Kristkindl* should have brought him another train."

Dad furrowed his brow. "Woman, we can't have this nonsense. No son of mine shall play with dolls. It would be a *Schande.*"

He pulled Joey to him, took his little hand and spoke to him, father to son. "Joey, it's Christmas, so I won't be angry with you, but I'll explain something: boys don't play with dolls. Never. Do you hear? The boys in my family become doctors, lawyers and engineers, and when they are asked, they fight for the *Vaterland*. Dolls are for girls. Do you hear me, Joey?  Do you understand, son?"

Joey lowered his head, his cheeks bathed in tears.

"He's overly excited and tired," pleaded Mom, taking Joey and hiding his face in her soft woolen skirt.

"Here, Joey, have your nice fluffy teddy," coaxed Auntie.

Joey choked back hiccups and stared at me with woeful eyes from behind Mom's skirts, his nose snotty from all the crying.  I was busy loving my beautiful doll.

"It's bedtime soon," said Mom.  She led us to the Christmas table full of cookies, cakes, and candied treats.  Joey forgot his sorrow for a while as he munched on honey and ginger cookies in the shape of trees, stars, angels and flowers.

After we had eaten, Mom took us to our little duvet beds. She put Joey's yellow teddy beside his pillow and my lovely doll by my side. My doll's eyelids were closed, but her lips were smiling as if she was having a beautiful dream.

"*Schlaft, meine Liebchen*," Mom whispered and gave us each a big hug.  She turned off the lights and slipped out of the room.

In the dark I could hear Joey sobbing softly.  In the living room, Mom, Dad and Auntie were chatting and clinking their glasses.

"Joey," I whispered in the dark, "I have an idea!"

Joey stopped sobbing.

Quietly, I slipped out of my bed and, perched on my toes, turned on the light.  Joey was sitting in his bed with his teddy dropped to the floor.

I went to him and said, "Do you want to hold my doll for a while? Would you like that, Joey?"

He nodded.  I carried my doll importantly to him.

"Can I see how her eyes open and close?" he asked.

"Sure.  But be gentle.  She is very delicate.  Her name is Lily."

I smiled because the name had just occurred to me.  It seemed the right name for a doll that looked like a friend.

Joey held Lily on his lap.  Ever so slowly, he tilted her head backwards.  The doll's eyelids fell shut.  When he raised her head, her eyelids opened again. He tested this phenomenon several times. Satisfied, he handed my doll back to me.

I turned off the light and tucked Lily in my bed. I slipped quietly beside her under my warm duvet. I stroked her silky hair and drifted into a contented sleep, thankful to *Kristkindl* for my wonderful gift.

Joey's yellow teddy bear spent most of his time in Dad's armchair while Dad was away at his office in Berlin. When Dad came back from Berlin, he gave Joey a bright red locomotive to make up for the disappointing Christmas present. I let Joey hold Lily once in a while so he could watch her eyes open and close. When he got tired of the doll's mechanism, he returned to his trains and wooden blocks. Lily was my special friend for a long time. I loved her so much that her hair grew thin, her colors faded, and her clothes turned to rags.
I don't remember what became of her. Perhaps she was left behind during our hectic travels, abandoned like so many of our possessions. I like to think that another little girl had the happiness to cherish her as I did.

*"Only the dead have seen the end of war."*
George Santayana
*"When the rich wage war, it's the poor who die."*
Jean-Paul Sartre

# A Strange Girl

One evening, after Auntie had settled down with her knitting -- Auntie was always knitting woolen socks and sweaters for us—I asked her, "Why can't I go to school like Elvira?"

"Elvira is a big girl and you are only five, Erika. You must wait another year."

"But you said I was smart!" I protested.

She looked at me through her thick glasses. "Don't be in such a hurry to go to school, little Erika!"

But I was in a hurry. I wanted to learn how to read. Words looked so intriguing: black squiggles in the Berlin newspapers Dad read with a frown and blue curls in the letters Mom read with tears. I wanted to learn their secret.

"Could you teach me the alphabet, Auntie?" I begged.

She shook her head. "That would be wrong, Erika. You must wait till your teacher teaches you."

"But Elvira said I will get the strap if I don't know my letters!"

"Elvira wanted to scare you. When you go to school, your teacher will show you the alphabet, one letter at a time. Besides, it does no harm to get a little beating once in a while. It gives you character."

"Auntie, did you ever get the strap when you were a little girl?"

"Yes. I got *Tatzen* once for not knowing a poem. But how could *Mutterle* afford a poetry book? We had lost our farm in the Depression. We had barely enough to eat."

Auntie's eyes got red whenever she mentioned *Mutterle*, my Bavarian great grand-mother, who had died long ago. I did not want to annoy her anymore, so I sat quietly and thought about all this.

When Auntie took me on the rear seat of her bicycle to buy a loaf of brown bread at Herr Mueller's-- the local baker, who had a lame leg and could not join the army-- I peeked at the little school house with its white washed walls and concrete steps. Sometimes, I glimpsed children skipping ropes or playing tag in the yard. They were having fun. When there was an air raid alarm, they ran home with their books in their arms and laughed because they got out of school early. I saw Elvira too, but she never played their games. During recess she stood quietly and alone under the lime trees of the yard and never ran and shouted like the other children.

Every school day morning, I watched her walk past our kitchen window in her faded grey coat, her tightly wound braids and her leather satchel strapped firmly to her back. A few times she turned her pale blue eyes in my direction, but I don't think she could see me through our lace curtains. She walked slowly and resolutely down the paved *Dorfstrasse* in front of our house and disappeared behind the leafy hedge of the school.

Elvira's mother, Frau Schiller, said that Elvira was the smartest student in her class and studied all the time. Frau Schiller was our neighbor in Braunsdorf, where we lived after our apartment in Berlin had been bombed. She visited our house every week to sell us eggs and vegetables from her farm. She was a rotund woman with bulging blue eyes. One of her eyelids had a nervous twitch. My mom felt sorry for her because her husband had died in Stalingrad, leaving her alone with three young children. Elvira often helped her carry the eggs and produce. Although Elvira was only ten, she was always serious and never smiled.

Once in a while, Auntie asked Elvira to look after Joey and me while she did the ironing or went to the grocery store for sugar and flour. Mom never had time for us. She was nursing my newborn sister Margie and looking after my twin sisters, Helga and Ute, who were crawling and putting everything in their mouth.

One day when Elvira came to our house, I asked her, "Elvira, did you ever get the strap?"

She looked at me with disgust. "Of course not. I always do my homework. When I am big I will be a doctor like your dad."

"Will you show me how to read?" I asked.

"May be, if you are good."

She took Joey and me to the meadow behind our house where no one could see us. "I must practice to be a doctor," she said. "You are my patients. You must do what I tell you."

She had such an air of authority that neither Joey nor I dared to contradict her.

She went about her task expertly. She stamped down a patch of grass to flatten it into pretend beds. Joey and I had to lie down and make believe that we had been injured. She made Joey tuck in his lower leg as if it had been blown off by a bomb. She had me pin one arm behind my back so that I had only one arm like Uncle Henry after he had been shot in Leningrad. She bandaged us with handkerchiefs and towels. She would also take a stick and pretend to saw off a limb. She said that doctors amputate the soldiers' limbs to prevent blood poisoning. She never hurt us. When we died, she closed our eyes and put daisies on our chest. She played these games quickly and secretly before Auntie could find her out.

Auntie did not like Elvira. She told Mom that Elvira was strange. A child that never laughs is not a right child, she said, and will come to no good. But Mom said that Elvira was serious and sensitive. I didn't know what "sensitive" meant but it sounded distinguished. Whenever the air raid alarm sounded, Elvira's ears ached so badly that she curled up on the ground and whimpered. Her mother stuffed cotton in her ears, but that did not help.

During the air raid alarms, Elvira's family rushed to our cement basement, which was larger and stronger than theirs. Everyone sat down in the darkness and listened for the sound of planes. After all was safe, Auntie opened the cellar door and we rushed outside into the daylight, happy that our houses were intact. But Elvira did not come with us. She stayed crouched in a corner with her hands over her ears. Her mother had to drag her out of the cellar to take her home.

I asked Auntie if I was sensitive. She laughed, "I can't say you are sensitive like most. You don't have ear aches like Elvira, and you don't scream like Joey when you are upset. Things sink into you quietly. They hide and may come out later like fish from a river."

"That's silly!" I laughed.

I had seen boys pull out grey fish from the canal behind our house. I squirmed thinking that ghostly fish swam inside me.

After we had played doctor, Elvira wanted to be alone so she could study her school book, but I pestered her about the alphabet. She refused to teach me at first, but after I had begged her several times, she decided to do me a favor because I had been a good patient. She took a pointed stick and traced A in the dust, then B, and C, and also numbers. I copied her tracings carefully, but she said they were not very good. Our lessons never got farther than H, which stood for hospital. I remembered it well for it looked like a bed. After babysitting us Elvira rushed home because she had to help her mother with her two little brothers.

I forgot about school for the following weeks. Something ominous was in the air. My mother and Auntie whispered with sighs and head shaking. They glanced out the windows with fear and even ran out on the porch to listen to something far away, a kind of rumble or shooting on the horizon where the sun rises.

One afternoon my Dad left his medical practice in Berlin and hurried home in a taxi. His face was flushed and his jaws tight. He walked briskly past Joey and me and headed straight for the bedroom where Mom was nursing my infant sister Margie and where my twin sisters, Helga and Ute, were sleeping. Although adults never shared their secrets with children, I knew from the hoarse whispers behind their bedroom door that something dangerous and urgent was about to happen.

Mom and Auntie were furiously packing utensils, clothes, beddings, photos, and even toys in large leather suitcases and cotton bags. Why were they packing our beddings? Frau Schiller, whose bad eye was twitching worse than ever, came with Elvira and her two little boys to pick up kitchen pots, towels, carpets and other items that Mom gave away because she said she did not need them anymore. Everyone acted very strange. They pushed Joey and me out of the house and called us in only for our mealtime.

Elvira came to look after us while Mom and Auntie continued packing.

"What is happening?" I asked her.

She looked at me in her serious way and explained, "You are going away because the Russians are coming. If you listen hard, you can hear them shooting." She pointed in the direction where Mom and Auntie were always looking.

I had overheard Dad say that our enemies would be cruel and dangerous. They would do horrible things to women and children, things that would make them bleed and die.

"Are you going away too?" I asked Elvira.

She shook her head. "My mother can't afford it. We'll run to the forest or hide in the swamp near the canal. They won't get us! Never!"

"I made a gift for you," she added quickly as if to change the subject. "It's a reward because you've been an excellent patient and a good student. Close your eyes, Erika!"

I closed my eyes.

I heard her fumble in the pockets of her faded apron.

"Guess!" she said.

"Is it marbles? Candies? Pictures?"

She said No repeatedly.

"Now you can look," she said. "It's something I made for you!"

She held out a small shoddy notebook she had pasted together out of the blank spaces in newspapers, and also gave me the stub of a pencil. I never had used a pencil before because Auntie was afraid that the twins, who were at the walking stage, would trip and hurt themselves on its sharp point.

"You can practice your letters so you won't get the strap," she said softly, and then quickly ran away so that I would not see that she was crying.

I turned her gifts over in my hands with a heavy heart.

That was the last time I saw Elvira-- Elvira with her ear aches and sad blue eyes.


Early at dawn the following day, under a grey sky and with no neighbors in sight, a horse and carriage took us to the main train station in Berlin. There, we said farewell to Dad, who had to stay behind to join the Fuehrer's last hopeless stand against the Allies. My dad, like many Germans, knew the war was nearly lost and had arranged for Mom, the children and Auntie to escape to Duens, a snowed in alpine village at the foot of the *Drei Schwestern* near Feldkirch in Austria.

We boarded the last train that left the devastated city and joined the many distraught refugees on the run throughout Europe. We learned later from other refugees of what had happened in Braunsdorf. The Russian soldiers had invaded the village and searched the forest with their guns. They had locked the inhabitants in basements, helped themselves to whatever food and goods they could find, but soon released most of the villagers, who after all were only women, children, and old folks, since all able bodied males were in the army. Some women and girls were raped, and some villagers tortured and killed, but no one wanted to give details. "The past is the past," they said. "There is no use looking back."


After the Berlin Wall had fallen, my mother and I returned to

Braunsdorf. We visited Herr Mueller, the old crippled baker whom we remembered well. He invited us for coffee and cake in his living quarters behind the bakery, which was filled with fresh loaves and buns and smelled as good as in the olden days. He introduced us to his son Kurt and his daughter-in-law, a jovial young couple, who owned the business now and served their many customers.

"What happened to the Schillers?" asked my mom after we had had our first cup of coffee and piece of *Torte*. "They were our neighbors when we lived here."

"They disappeared," said the old baker. " When the Russians came with their guns, everyone ran to the forest to hide. Some Russians stayed in Schiller's farm before invading Berlin. Then the East Germans moved in. The communists gave them Schiller's farm. They gave them also your house and your property near the canal."

"But what happened to Frau Schiller and her three children?" my mother insisted.

"They disappeared. May be they were taken to Siberia. May be they escaped to the west. I have my theory..."

"What do you mean?" asked my mother.

"The canal," said the old man, his pale eyes so blurry they were almost white. "Women were afraid to be raped and have their children raped. That was the victors' way. Someone thought they had seen Frau Schiller and Elvira pitch the boys' bodies in the canal at night. They may have poisoned or sedated them. It would not surprise me. Elvira was a strange girl. The mother and daughter threw themselves in the water afterwards. Who knows? They weren't the only ones. The Leonard wife drowned her baby in a tub and hung herself. A hell of a time! The devil had his way!"

The old man shook his head as if he wanted to clear his mind of terrible memories. My mother looked away without a word. I knew she was thinking of what would have happened to us if Dad had not helped us escape in time. I remembered Elvira and her sad little gift. She wanted to be a doctor. It was not meant to be.

"Thank God, it's over!" muttered the old man and smiled again as he offered us another piece of his delicious *Torte*.

The war was a grotesque nightmare best forgotten.

*"War does not determine who is right-- only who is left."*
*Bertrand Russell*

# Cousins in Fuerstenwalde

**W**hen we escaped from Berlin, we left behind sad and tragic memories. Was there anything I could have said or done in my five year old wisdom to prevent the disaster that befell my two little cousins, children my age, whom I remember staring at me with curious and woeful eyes in their home in Fuerstenwalde?

I still can see them in their spotless white kitchen with an enamel stove and cooler, and matching cupboards. Dig as I may into my memory, I remember little else. The whole horrid tale, full of assumptions and conjectures was retold in my family many times. It was mostly Mom, with her large compassionate eyes, who told the tale, relaying every detail of the tragedy, feeling fortunate that it had not occurred to her and her babies on that fateful day of 1945 when the Russians crossed the Oder-Spree Canal and invaded Braunsdorf, a village east of Berlin, where we used to live.

My two little cousins, a boy and a girl, whom I was too shy to approach, lived in their house in Fuerstenwalde with their mother, Auntie Hewig. Their young father had been enlisted to fight on the Russian front. Auntie Hedwig had not heard of him for over a year. She feared the worst.

Auntie Hedwig was young and beautiful. Her hair was darker than that of her sisters, Rete and Marie, Dad's unmarried sisters and his receptionists at his medical practice in Berlin. To my youthful eyes she seemed grandiose and elegant, more refined than my other uneducated aunts who had spent their youth on their farm in Landshut. She was a pharmacist by profession, an unusual feat for a woman of rural lineage. With her husband she owned her business in Fuerstenwalde. She was highly respected in her community but somewhat outcast by her jealous sisters, who had not had the opportunity to go to university. It was not considered proper in this World War II era for German women to devote themselves to careers other than *Hausfrau* and motherhood.

My mother excelled in both. Married at twenty to my father, a mature doctor of thirty-five, she proceeded at once to produce babies on a yearly basis. At the age of five I was the eldest of five children, with my mother expecting a sixth. My mother was the wonderful Germanic prototype, tall, blond, healthy, shy and submissive. She was a descendent of the Grimhildes of the Rhine region, the Leonores of the Romantics, the mother of the future Teutonic race of the Third Reich. I am being ironic, but those were the fantasies of German men at one time. Auntie told me that she was just the type my father was looking for when he met her at Garmisch, a holiday resort in Bavaria. My mother secretly despised the government's propaganda and pretentiousness, but in her position as a *Hausfrau* she had no choice but to blindly trust my father. Perhaps that is why she secretly envied women like her sister-in-law Hedwig and her own sister Ulla, a medical student, who were not dependent on men for their livelihood.

My mother was naturally compassionate and empathetic. She was capable of monumental suffering, as she proved later on. Why on the evening of her visit in Fuerstenwalde could she not foresee and forestall the gruesome events which were to ensue? Why could she not lure this proud, intelligent and misguided woman away from her home and urge her to join us in our flight to Austria?

The Russians were advancing on Berlin. My mother said that shooting could be heard east of Braunsdorf where we were residing. Rumors circulated that Hitler had lost his battles on the eastern front and was losing the west. My father followed the war secretly on clandestine British broadcasts and knew the truth. He came to our summerhouse in Braunsdorf, outside of Berlin, and arranged train tickets for us. He urged us to leave at once with whatever we could bundle up. "The Russians are coming! They will destroy all on their path! The Russians are sending their Mongols to rape children and kill women. You must flee at once."

One early winter morning, when it was still dark outside, I was rushed out of bed and dressed up in as many clothes as I could wear under my coat. My little brother Joey, my little twin sisters, Helga and Ute, and my new baby sister Margie were bundled up in the same manner and ushered into a horse drawn carriage that took us to the Berlin train station. It was so dark I could not see the horse, but I knew it was there, taking us away. Our luggage consisted mostly of feather ticks and suitcases with clothing and kitchen pots that Auntie and Mom had packed the previous days. To ensure that nothing would get lost, they had wrapped devotedly a wooden statue of the Madonna in the bedding. My little brother Joey was howling like always when he sensed anxiety. I was silent and docile for I knew that any questions on my part would be met with annoyance. Mom and Auntie were in a nervous frenzy and made sure that the children and luggage were loaded securely. I was squeezed on the front bench of the cart between the driver and Auntie Rete, who was also watching the children in the back. Mom followed behind with the baby buggy loaded with bags and Auntie Voit carried two enormous suitcases. I must have fallen asleep, for I do not remember our flight in the dark.

The next thing I remember is that we arrived at the train station in the midst of a crowd of panicked people, who were shouting and shoving. Auntie, with suitcases and bundles in the twins' baby carriage, got separated from Mom, who was holding baby Margie and had Joey and me clinging to her coat while her sister-in-law Rete was carrying the restless twins. My father, who was waiting for us at the station, pushed my mother and Auntie Rete with the five children into the overcrowded train. People gave us seats near a window.

It was broad daylight by then. My bladder was irritating me. I remember the train and its nervous passengers through this childish detail. My red face went through contortions in fear of an accident. My little brother had the same problem, but being a boy, Mom helped him to relieve himself out of the window. But this was not possible for me. Some women took pity on my grimaces and suggested that I be "lifted" to the toilet. The alleys in the train were packed so tightly that not even a mouse could have gone through. Mercifully, I was hoisted over the heads of passengers until I reached the washroom.

These are some recollections of our flight out of Berlin in February 1945. My father could not come with us because he had been called to the front. In his foresight, he had made sure that we should escape Berlin. But why did he not provide for his sister Hedwig and her two children? Why did he not force them to leave? Why did they face the horror of the enemy's invasion, rape and plunder?

I was told later that Hedwig had refused to leave because she wanted to wait for her husband's return. Why did she stay and risk her life and her children's? Was she too proud to accept help from her unfriendly sisters whom she had outdistanced in education and elegance? Was she fearful of rejection? Why was the poor misguided woman alone in Fuerstenwalde when the Russians with their Mongol tribes advanced on Berlin?

My mother says that Hedwig and the children ran with other townspeople to hide in the woods and that they may have been caught and taken as prisoners to Russian camps. Her husband returned safely after the war. For many years he searched the town, the forest and the entire country but found no trace of them. With sadness and bitterness he lived out his life, never remarried, and never experienced joy again. His notices for missing persons in newspapers all over the world remained unanswered.

In moments of reflection, my mother said that Hedwig and her children were not captured by the Russians at all, but drowned in the Oder-Spree canal to escape the barbaric horrors of defeat— a time when little girls walked down the streets with blood dripping from their legs. Also Hedwig was a pharmacist and might have resorted to an overdose of sedatives. Someone reported having seen an ambulance near her home.

This is a family story that weighs heavily on our conscience to this day. My family escaped to Austria where we found refuge. Auntie, with our luggage securely tied up in the baby carriage, found us in the air raid shelter in Munich where my mother had given her a hasty rendezvous. She had boarded another train that had followed ours. We all reached Austria where we were safe from the horrible events ensuing in Berlin. But so many like Hedwig and her children succumbed to the despair of a defeated Germany.

*"In modern war...you will die like a dog for no good reason."*
                                            *Ernest Hemingway*
*"War is a defeat for humanity."*
                                            *Pope John Paul II*

# Under the Apple Tree

*Duens, Austria, 1945*

On the back of a yellowish photograph in our family album I read in my mother's neat handwriting: *Duens, 1945*. Our family was gathered under the leafy branches of an apple tree: the snow patched Alps outlined in one corner, the white wall of a house on the other side. How our lives had changed! How confused and lost were we in the war's aftermath!

In the back row, my young mother, beautiful in a flowery dress, was cuddlling her new baby Pueppi (Beate). Beside her, my dad in a formal suit and his old aunt, both wearing glasses, were staring earnestly into the camera. In the front row, we children were squirming in the sunshine: my little sisters -- Helga, Ute,and Margie -- and I, in the same grey frocks and white bows, and Joey in shorts, with his hair so blond that it looked white. I don't remember on which occasion this picture was taken or by whom, but I remember well the apple tree.

In February 1945, my dad had arranged our escape from Berlin to Duens, a remote Austrian village on the slopes of the Alps, where we would be sheltered from the disastrous bombings of the Allies. He also feared the end of the war, Germany's defeat and its terrible aftermath, which he believed to be inevitable.

He could not come with us for he had been recruited -- like all other male civilians, including boys-- to fight the advancing Russian troops. It was a hopeless mission, but he had no choice. He had to pick up an infantry rifle (he would never shoot) and join the German army on the eastern front. Fortunately, he had taken out his savings before the German banks crashed and handed over his entire money, hidden in a suitcase, to my mom before she boarded the train that took us out of Berlin.

When we arrived in Feldkirch, we were overwhelmed by the heaps of snow that surrounded us. We children had never seen so much snow. A steep winding road led up to the village Duens. There was no public transportation, so we proceeded on foot, three women (Auntie Rete was still with us) and five small children. I remember slipping and falling in my leather boots while the little ones cried and wanted to be carried. A kind Austrian came along with his sled pulled by a horse. After greeting us with a cheery *"Gruess Gott!"* he offered to take us and our luggage up the hill.

Thanks to dad's money we could afford the village hotel for a few days, but when my mom looked for a place to rent, she found that the local villagers were reluctant to let us stay in their houses. We could not blame them: we were the hated Germans who had annexed their country. Eventually my mom and Auntie's religious faith touched the local priest and his pious house keeper; they rented us the lower floor of their spacious parish house. We children played quietly indoors while Mom and Auntie cooked our gruel and potato soups on the cast iron stove of the priest's kitchen.

My pregnant mom and Auntie (Dad's aunt) were in constant anxiety about Dad. They tried to find out from rumors at the grocery store and at church after mass, what was going on in Germany. Everywhere they heard tales of horror about the terrible destruction in the cities, the flight and misery of inhabitants, the lack of food and medical aid. Every day they prayed to our wooden statue of the Madonna, which we had brought along from Berlin, that Dad would be spared on the front. Around Eastertime Mom received a postcard that informed her that Dad had been taken prisoner, but she did not know where and by whom; she feared that he had been transported, like so many German soldiers, to the Russian labor camps in Siberia. Dad told us later that he had miraculously escaped from a Russians make-shift camp, but had been recaptured by the Americans.

With the arrival of spring the snow melted, the alpine meadows turned a deep green and cowbells tingled in the hills. Mom and Auntie hung their laundry in the priest's garden, while we children rolled in the sweet smelling grass or chased each other around the fruit trees in the yard.

The war was coming to an end. Many refugees came into the town. Mom and Auntie warned us that we must stay close to the parish house, not venture beyond the fence, and never speak to strangers.

I was the eldest and had to watch over my little brother and sisters.

Early one morning— I cannot remember the month as I did not go to school yet —I was standing barefoot under the apple tree in the parish yard when the sun burst over the mountain peaks and threw diamonds on the leaves. We had been so boisterous at breakfast that Auntie had shooed us outdoors.

My brother and little sisters were squealing with delight to see the abundance of apples strewn in the meadow after the storm of the previous night. They were picking apples out of the dewy grass, biting into them and tossing them about in their childish way.

I found an enormous green apple and chewed its white flesh down to its brown kernels. I was wiping the juice dripping from my chin when I looked up and saw a dusty vagabond walking along the path that lead to our parish house. This struck me as odd as no one except our neighbors ever came to see us. There was something vaguely familiar in his long determined gait, in the way he held his head and swung his arms. His face was partly hidden under a brimmed hat and his emaciated shape seemed to vanish in the dusty folds of a loose and shabby coat. He looked about as if he were searching for something. When he spied us under the apple tree, he rushed toward us. I dropped my apple, and with my heart beating wildly, I stared into his pale stubbly face and frosty blue eyes behind steel rimmed glasses.

Suddenly he lunged at two year old Margie and whisked her off her feet. The child screamed in terror and kicked mightily. He tried to pick up Helga and Ute, my twin sisters, but they were clinging to my skirt with howls and shrieks. My little brother Joey, who knew no better, began to wail while I watched perturbed this confusion of cries and tears. The stranger put down my little sisters, hesitated as if confused and slowly backed away.

The door of our white parish house burst open and Auntie flew out with a shriek. She ran toward the stranger and shouted at him. I thought she would shoo him away, but instead, she patted his hands and laughed and wept at the same time. I did not understand what they were saying. It was grown up talk beyond my experience. Auntie pulled the stranger by the hand and led him back to us. She bent down to our height and shook her gnarly finger into our tear stained faces. I remember to this day her scolding words, *"Das ist euer Vater, ihr dumme Kinder!"* "That's your father, you dumb children!"

My eight month pregnant mother, alerted by the commotion, came running down the stairs so fast that she tripped over her slippers and injured her ankle. She hobbled towards my father. I will always remember her flushed face and the tears that rolled down her cheeks as she threw her arms around his neck.

I understood nothing about the end of the war and the release of German prisoners from American POW camps, but that day I sensed that something wonderful had happened.

Mom told me later that Dad had made it a point to arrive in time for her birthday on July 14th. My new baby sister Beate was born a month later. Mom was grateful all her life that her prayers had been answered and that Dad had returned safely. Many of the German soldiers and prisoners-of-war never saw their families again.

*"I've learned that people will forget what you said, people will forget what you did, but people will never forget how you made them feel."*

*Maya Angelou*

# The Circus

After Dad was released from an American prisoners' camp, he joined us for a few months in the village of Duens in Austria, where we had taken refuge. Everyone and everything was very confused. Germany was in tatters and divided up among the Allies. Berlin was demolished and starving. Dad did not want to go back to his medical practice in Germany. He would have liked to go overseas, to America or Brazil, like two other German doctors in the village; however, his savings were insufficient to cover the travel expenses for six children and three adults. Auntie, who had been his nanny when he was little, was included in all our family plans.

France needed laborers, so Dad decided to cross the border and hire himself out as a farmhand for minimal wages. Mom, who was pregnant again, remained in Austria with Auntie and the children until she would be able to get the necessary visas to join him.

Mom was only twenty seven and still very young at heart. She loved us dearly, her six little ones, and tried to make the best out of our strained circumstances. She took us on outings in the mountains where we could run wildly among the alpine grasses and flowers and pick berries. At night, when she was not too tired from nursing Beate, she amused us with fairy tales and Bible stories.

When she heard that a circus with large animals was coming to Innsbruck, she planned to take us there, but she kept her intentions a secret so as not to break out little hearts if she should not be able to afford this luxury.

One morning, when it was still dark outside, I heard a noise in the kitchen and got up. Flies were buzzing in the dim light and throwing shadows as big as birds on the walls. But the most amazing sight was Auntie standing on a kitchen chair and trying to thread a needle near the ceiling light bulb. With her long bony arms and wrinkled legs, she looked like the woodpecker that had been hammering on our neighbor's tree. I burst out laughing.

She stared at me through her thick glasses and snarled, "Erika, you naughty girl! You ungrateful pest! Mocking me when I'm helping your poor mother with you, kids!"

She spat out the word 'kids' as if we were a pack of rats.

She was a good helper to Mom, but she was often in a foul mood.

"If you show me what you're doing, I can help you," I said.

She climbed off her chair and thrust her needle at me. I threaded it within seconds  and handed it back to her. She sat down with Joey's coat.

"You never sew so early, Auntie," I said in a conciliatory tone. "What are you doing with Joey's coat?"

"Sewing on buttons, silly! That stupid boy rips everything!"

I looked around.  Our porridge was simmering on the cast iron stove and our table was set for breakfast. We never ate so early.

"What's going on, Auntie?"

"You are off to Innsbruck this morning!"

"Are we going to the photographer's again?" We had gone to Innsbruck recently to have our pictures taken for visas; Mom wanted to join my dad in southern France.

"No. No photos. Your mom is taking you to a circus. Our landlady, Frau Scholler, gave us tickets last night because she couldn't go herself. Your foolish mom!  Taking you to a circus when your dad's away, and there is hardly enough money to feed you! And her expecting again!"

Auntie always made us feel guilty. She was constantly complaining about our noise and mess and never wanted us to have fun. But I was excited. I raced into Mom's bedroom, where the little ones were sleeping in her bed, and cried, "Mom, is it true? Are we going to the circus?"

Mom rubbed her eyes and gave me a big smile. My little brother Joey, who had heard the word 'circus', started to scream, "I want to see the elephants! I want to see the elephants!"

Mom was pink with happiness, "Yes, Erika, we're going to the circus, but we must hurry. We must catch the early bus to Innsbruck."

I helped her dress my four year old sisters, Helga and Ute, in their matching dresses, woolen stockings and booties. Joey was flushed with excitement. He ran into the kitchen and gulped down his porridge. He wanted to leave right away. He even got his shoes on the right feet, so that Auntie only had to tie up his shoelaces.

After breakfast Mom packed several bottles of lemonade and some jam sandwiches in a large brown rucksack she carried over her shoulders. Auntie stayed home with three year old Margie and one year old Beate. When we left she was still muttering that it was nonsense to drag four small children to the city to see stupid animals and silly clowns. But Mom ignored her reprimands and thanked her cheerily for watching the babies.

Bundled up in our coats and bonnets, we happily followed our mom downhill along twisting alleys, past wooden farmhouses and stables, through apple orchards and fields until we reached the bus stop on the main road. Pink clouds floated over the snowy peaks of the Alps. It promised to be a marvelous day.

Several people wrapped in felt coats and woolen shawls were clustered at the bus stop. They were chatting and craning their necks. Soon, a small bus rattled around a corner. The driver, wearing a black shiny visor, stepped out importantly and checked the tickets of the passengers. When it was Mom's turn, he said coldly, "Madam, you are only allowed two children for free. You have to pay for the other two."

He told her how much it would cost to go to Innsbruck. Mom blushed. She looked at my twin sisters. It was too late to take them back to Auntie. She stepped to the side and poked nervously at the coins in her wallet. A finely dressed lady, who had overheard the bus driver, took my mom aside. "I'm going to Innsbruck too. I have no children," she added sweetly, "I'll pretend these two are mine. " She pointed at my brother and me. Mom thanked her and we boarded the bus without trouble.

We took four seats in the back. Mom took Helga on her lap and had Ute and Joey share the seat beside her. I got to sit across the aisle beside the beautiful lady who had pretended I was her daughter. She had told my mom before boarding the bus that she had gone to the village to look for a summer cottage in the Alps for the health of her husband.

I looked her over carefully, her shiny dark curls that smelled of roses, her glossy red lips, her manicured nails that rested softly on her flowery silken dress. My mother never wore make-up or perfume. Auntie was ugly and full of wrinkles. The stranger seemed an exotic creature from another world. In her delicately shaped ears she wore golden hoops with sparkling stones.

She turned towards me. Her dark velvety eyes under thinly drawn eyebrows caressed mine.

"You like my earrings?"

"They are very beautiful."

"They are diamonds," she said.

She pushed one of my braids aside and said, "You have pretty ears. I'll give you earrings with blue stones to match your eyes. You are a very pretty girl, did you know that?"

I smiled very pleased. No one had ever told me I was pretty. Auntie always told me that I was nasty and ugly. She did not believe in spoiling girls with compliments. And Mom was too busy with babies to notice one way or another.

"You go to school?" asked the pretty lady.

"Yes. I can read and write a little."

The pretty lady nodded thoughtfully.

"Where is your dad?" she asked.

"He went away to work on a French farm."

"So, your mom lives alone with the children?"

"No. She has Auntie to help her."

"Your mom is lucky to have so many healthy children. My husband was injured in the war. Now we can't have children. Would you like to visit me some time?"

"If my mom allows."

The beautiful lady took my hand and said, "You will like my home. I have a big house with a fountain and many roses. In the garden there is a swing where you can swing so high that you can see the whole city. I also have a doll house."

"With real dolls?"

"Yes. Some as tall as you."

I looked up in wonder. I had only paper dolls and rag dolls I had made myself. This lady must be from a fairyland. Across the aisle I could hear my twin sisters fight over a toy and my mother scold my brother who was running back and forth down the aisle.

In Innsbruck the bus came to a halt. All the passengers went out. The beautiful lady approached my mom and said, "I will meet you after the circus. I have something very important to ask you." She winked at me.

"How will you find me? There are so many people!" said my mom.

"I will find you," said the pretty lady and smiled.

I forgot all about the beautiful lady when I heard the exciting music resounding from the colorful circus tent. We found seats in the front row. The show started with lights flashing and sounds bursting from every direction. Clowns with big red noses and polka dot suits chased each other and squirted water at us. My little twin sisters shrieked in terror and hid in Mom's skirt. There were acrobats and fire-eaters, monkeys in droll hats, horses with fancy plumes, gorgeous ladies with little dogs that jumped through hoops, and many other delights. If someone had asked me what I wanted to be, I would have replied without hesitation, a circus girl who could fly on a trapeze and do somersaults on a horse's back. I wished I had long black hair instead of my skinny blond braids and a fancy glittery dress instead of my dull grey coat and woolen bonnet.

My brother jumped up and down and pointed at the red curtains. In lumbered three majestic elephants with crimson carpets on their backs and golden tassels down their foreheads. A man in white silken pants guided the troupe. The elephants held each other's tails, stepped on stools, and did amazing tricks, their trunks and mighty tusks in the air, their mouths open in a grin.

For the finale the man invited several children to ride on one of the elephants that had a basket attached to its back. To my amazement he came towards me and held out his hand. I hesitated, but my mom laughed. "Go on!" she encouraged me and gave the man a coin. Trembling, I followed the man. My little brother howled and stamped his feet, "I want to ride the elephant! I want to ride the elephant!"

The man smiled and took my little brother's hand and said to my mom, "You don't need to pay for him." He helped us both up the ladder into the elephant's howdah. We sat with other children on a little bench. I felt dizzy and was afraid to look down. The elephant lumbered along. I clung fearfully to the edge of my seat as it rocked from side to side. Joey was fearless. He stood up on the bench and waved at my mother and twin sisters. I tried to pull him back down.

"I am proud of you!" beamed Mom when we dismounted.

After the show the crowd headed for the doors. Mom watched us carefully so as not to lose us. Joey could not stop chatting about the elephants, while Helga and Ute were whimpering because they were hungry. Mom looked for a park where we could have our picnic.

She headed for a bench under oak trees. She opened her knapsack and served us lemonade and jam sandwiches. While we were devouring our food, we saw the fine lady saunter toward us, her silken skirt swaying lightly and the feathers on her stylish hat waving in the breeze. She came to our bench and smiled at us. Mom blushed, embarrassed-- the twins had jam all over their cheeks. The elegant lady said, "Please, don't stop, *liebe Frau!* Keep feeding the children!"

She looked at me. "Did you enjoy the circus, Erika?" she asked in her musical voice.

"Oh yes," I replied.

"I rode an elephant!" cried Joey.

"That must have been very special," said the beautiful lady. She turned to my mom. "How many children do you have?"

"I have these four and two babies at home."

"It must be difficult to feed and care for so many little ones with your husband away." She paused meaningfully, "in these difficult times..."

Mom looked at her with a frown and said, "I have my husband's aunt to help me."

"Life does not seem fair," said the beautiful lady. "You have so many children and I have none. Why don't you give me Erika? I want so much to have a little girl!"

Mom grew pale and her lips trembled. "I cannot give away my children. I love them all."

The beautiful lady said, "Of course you love them. I see you are expecting again." Mom's head dropped. She put her hand to her swollen side.

The lady said brightly, "My husband and I will give Erika a fine home and a good education. She will have whatever she wants."

She took my hand. Her velvety eyes held mine, "Wouldn't you like that, Erika? Play with real dolls, learn ballet and music?"

"She is my daughter," cried Mom in a broken voice. "I can't give my children much but I do my best."

The beautiful lady held my hand and spoke sweetly. "I would not steal her. You could come with her siblings and see her whenever you wanted. But my husband and I would give her opportunities, which she obviously will never have in her present circumstances. I am sure her father would agree."

Mom's face turned a deep red that spread down to her neck. I saw her tighten her jaws and clench her fists. She took a quick step towards the fine lady as if she wanted to push her away, but she hesitated, struck by a sudden thought. She turned to me with her tender blue eyes that had comforted me so often. "Erika,' she said with a slight tremble in her voice, "I don't have the right to decide your future. You will always be my little girl and I will always love you, but this lady and her husband are offering you what I cannot give you. They will teach you music and dancing and give you a good education. Do you think you can leave us for a little while and learn all that?"

I thought of the beautiful circus girls, their graceful movements and happy smiles. I remembered Auntie who had often said I was *wuest*, ugly. I thought of the noise and confusion at home, my brother and sisters fighting, and my mom so tired and sad since my dad had gone away.

Joey and my twin sisters Helga and Ute stopped biting into their jam sandwiches and stared at me solemnly as if they sensed the enormity of my decision. I dared not look at Mom but I knew she was standing beside me, watching and waiting patiently.

The beautiful lady's fingers tightened around my wrist. I heard her fine bracelets jingle and smelled her rose perfume. "Well, Erika," she insisted in her musical voice.

I looked up into her velvety eyes with long lashes under thinly arched eyebrows, at her red painted lips and scented black curls, and deep in my heart, I panicked. I would not be home anymore to eat porridge with my brother and sisters and hear Mom tell fairy tales. I would not see the new baby when it was born. I would live in a strange house with a lady and a man I did not know.

The fine lady seemed to have guessed my thoughts. She lowered her voice in a soft purr, almost a whisper. "I will be good to you, little Erika, you'll see! Stay with me for a little while and then you can decide. What do you say?"

I shook my head, and doing so, I shivered a little as if I was cold. "I'm going home," I mumbled and looked up at Mom whose face lit up as if a light was shining inside her.

The beautiful lady nodded thoughtfully and let go of my hand. "I understand, little Erika," she murmured. "But you may regret your decision later on!"

She looked wistfully at me and stroked my head, then briskly turned around and walked down the road, her skirt swaying and her high heels clicking on the stony pavement.

Mom gave me a warm squeeze, then deftly packed our picnic things into her brown knapsack and rushed us to the bus station. I never saw the beautiful lady again, but I still remember the flash of her diamond earrings as she turned her head before stepping into a taxi.

*"Peace cannot be achieved through violence, it can only be attained through understanding."*

*Ralph Waldo Emerson*

# Red Nails

Dad had returned briefly to Berlin after the war. He had been horrified to see the city demolished and plundered, the people hungry and discouraged, his medical office in ruins and our house in the eastern sector inhabited by communists. He swore never to return.

He had found a temporary job as a farmhand near Tarbes, in southern France. This job permitted him to bring us over from Austria, where we had waited out the end of the war. After leaving us to fend for ourselves in a rented house in a village near the Pyrenees, he went to Paris, partly to settle his war shattered nerves, and partly to study at the Sorbonne and meet the requirements for a French medical license. He was hoping to practice medicine in France, but eventually found it was impossible.

Mom remained alone with Auntie and her seven young children in southern France. She supplemented our meager family allowance by sewing clothes for the local villagers.

"Your dad is coming to visit. You must be very good and quiet; he is not well," Mom told us after dinner before retreating to her sewing room. She had to meet an urgent deadline for a wedding and was very tired.

Auntie, who was part of our family, always reminded us that we would have been happy and rich if it had not been for the war, the big war whose ghastly ghost was following us like a shapeless devouring monster. It had destroyed our home and our dad's medical practice in Berlin. It had driven us through Europe on trains, coaches, horse carts, and on foot, from town to town, till we landed here in Fontrailles, a pleasant village at the foot of the Pyrenees, with the sky shining warmly, birds singing in fruit trees, and wild roses growing on hedges.

I was happy in this village where my mom's friendly manner won over her neighbors, Odette Fauque, the young school teacher who lived across the street with her little son Jacquie, and Sylvia Maumus and Irene Regis, the two farm wives down the road, who expected her to settle their feuds.

I did not really miss Dad. I had hardly ever seen him when I was little in Germany and in Austria. I hated it when Auntie reminded me of the war and how it had destroyed Dad's practice. I wanted to be free and happy in my childish way.

When Mom told us that Dad would visit us, I felt uneasy for I remembered his outbursts of frustration and anger. I never had seen him truly relaxed. When he did laugh it was a brutal roar at incidents whose humor escaped me. A savage beast seemed to live inside him, ready to tear out without warning. Mom said the horrors of the war in Berlin had unsettled him. Mom, Auntie, and the children had stayed in the relative safety of the suburbs while he had been exposed for five years to the constant bombardments, shelling, and conflagrations in the city. He chose to continue his medical practice under these dire circumstances rather than join the army and fight on the dreaded eastern front. He was an educated, peace loving man who had never shot a gun. His initial enthusiasm and faith in Hitler had been shattered. The brutality and hopelessness of the war had hit him to the core and confused him; it had destroyed his business and his plans for a prosperous future.

Disturbed by a vague premonition, I rushed up the wooden stairs to the attic where I had my dollhouse. My dollhouse was my treasure. I had made it out of a cardboard box in which I had installed floors and partitions. I had furnished it with shells of hazelnuts, walnuts and acorns, which served as bowls, chairs and beds. On its floors I had placed carpets of woven grass and tiny pots of flowers and pinecones. But my greatest treasures were my dolls. My mom could not afford toys, so I sewed my own miniature dolls with scraps of material that dropped from her Singer sewing machine. I made them out of material of all colors: black, yellow, red and white — an international, ethnic population. I embroidered their faces with eyes and mouths, and endowed their heads with woolen hair. I also added body parts which shocked my prudish mother. She raised her eyebrows, wondering about my moral health. But to me it seemed natural for women to have breasts to feed their babies and for men to be equipped like my little brother. My dolls ate, drank, slept, drove matchbox cars, and read miniature books like real little people.

The previous Christmas my dad had brought us candies wrapped in colorful red paper. I had salvaged these lovely transparent bits of paper in a special box. I took out the plastic scraps of paper and smoothed them out with my hands, wondering how I could use them. I dreamt of being a lady, a real lady like Camille who was a fashion model in Paris and who had returned to her family in Fontrailles for the holidays. My mom had sewn her a strapless yellow dress. The dress intrigued me immensely. I asked Mom how it stayed up without pins. Mom laughed but would not reveal the secret. My admiration for the beautiful model was boundless. I watched her glide elegantly like a swan into Mom's sewing room, her dark curly head held high, and her slim fingers with red nails clasping a magazine to discuss the famous Paris couturiers' latest creations, *dernier cri de Paris*.

There was a broken mirror on the wall in the attic. I stood on tiptoes and checked my babyish eight year old face. I sucked in my cheeks and made my lips into a red heart. I opened my pale blue eyes wide so that they were like Camille's sparkling chestnut eyes. I smoothened back my braided hair to make myself look more elegant, and walked about on my toes as if I were wearing high heels. I even dabbed my face with a touch of white flour that I had stolen from the kitchen. The red candy wrappers gave me an idea. I took the transparent paper and put it over my lips but it would not stick. I took scissors and cut out small ovals and stuck them with spit to my nails.

Thus attired, I sashayed downstairs, one step at a time like an elegant model out of a Parisian magazine. I held out my hands so that the pretty red papers would not slip off my nails. I did not see my father who had just entered the house and stood at the base of the stairs. Unshaven and ragged, he was staring at me through his round glasses with an odd expression. His cold blue eyes fixed me attentively. I froze on the step where I was standing.

"What's going on in this house?" he growled and rushed at me. He dragged me down the stairs by my arms and pulled me into the kitchen. He examined my nails. He shouted at Mom to come at once. Terrified, I began to scream. Mom ran out of her sewing room, wide eyed and alarmed, with my younger brother and sisters in tow.

"What are you teaching her?" my dad screamed. His face was livid. "The child is a *Luder*! Is that why I took you out of Berlin before the Russians did their abominations? Tell me! Is that why I saved you from hell? Look at her! Look what she's done, the hussy!"

I stood frozen and terrified. I did not know what he was talking about. I had done nothing wrong. Mom pleadingly tugged at Dad's arm. "She's only a child. It's only paper! It comes off!" She rubbed my fingers. "See, it is all off! She's only a little girl!"

"I've seen little girls in Berlin, little harlots standing by the lamp posts, luring foreign soldiers for a piece of bread. My God! I've seen little girls raped and bleeding! Let me give her a lesson for her own good!"

He lifted me by my shoulders and dragged me to the fireplace. "I will teach you! I will teach you! *Luder*!" Paralyzed with fear I was limp like a rag in his hands. My brother and little sisters were screaming. Mom, flushed and trembling, shouted to bring him to his senses. "Josef! Josef! She's just playing a game. Leave her alone!" But he did not listen. He reached for a sizable twig in the wooden crate and brandished it over me.

Mom hung on to his arm. "Josef! Josef! Let her go! She's your child." The red bits of paper that my mother had brushed off were sticking to my white apron. I must have looked miserable with my braids undone and my tear stained face. He let go of me. He looked around, highly bewildered, and dropped his stick in the burning fireplace. I saw him swallow hard and slink out of the kitchen. His heavy boots shuffled dully on the stairs. Mom followed him into her bedroom and spoke soothing words. My little brother and little sisters stopped crying and returned to their games.

That night, when Mom came to my bed to tuck me in, she whispered in my ear. "You must forgive your dad," she said. "When he was in Berlin, he saw horrible things. Little things can trigger terrible memories. You must forgive him, darling! He is not well. He does love you, you know."

I did not understand how Dad could be sick when he did not have a fever and did not cough. In my young mind, the war had happened a long time ago in a city far away. We did not hear war planes and there were no air raids anymore. I did not understand why the war was still haunting us like a recurring nightmare in this peaceful sunny village.

For many years I felt uneasy about my poor dad, who was trying so hard to find a safe homeland for his large family, a peace loving country that would protect us from wars, and at the same time, give him the opportunity to resume his profession and provide for us. I did not understand how his nerves had been shattered and how he had come to suffer such terrible psychic wounds. Only much later, when I was an adult and had children of my own, could I reminisce on past events with an understanding and forgiving heart.

*"Let there be work, bread, water and salt for all."*

*Nelson Mandela*

*"It has often been too easy for rulers and governments to incite man to war."*

*Lester B. Pearson*

# Bread or Cake

After five years of frustrating attempts to get his medical license in France, Dad heard from an acquaintance in Paris that Canada was looking for doctors. Canada was a vast country and much to his liking. He headed there immediately and found a job as an intern in a hospital in Winnipeg, Manitoba. A year later he arranged for Mom, Auntie and the children to join him in their new homeland where they would find peace and comfort, away from their bitter war time memories.

Mom and Auntie packed excitedly our belongings, and with six of us children (the two youngest remained temporarily with Mom's parents) they bravely crossed the Atlantic to join my dad in Winnipeg in May 1953.

It was our last day on the ship. The Columbia of the Greek Line had docked in the harbor of Quebec City. The passengers were asked over the intercom to return to their cabins after they had finished breakfast.

At breakfast Mom was both excited and apprehensive. Occasionally she giggled nervously at the prospect of entering a new country and being reunited with her husband after a year's absence. At other times she felt glum at the knowledge that her wallet was empty and her children hungry. She wondered with Auntie, my father's aunt, if her husband Josef had sent a money order to Quebec as he had promised. In any case she decided that excitement was better than apprehension. She ate and laughed cheerily while urging her children to down as much food as they could, as they might not be having lunch or dinner for a while. Very slyly, she slipped a few buns from the breakfast table into her large purse, for she was sure that this good country did not grow bread on trees. The breakfast was especially sumptuous as it was the anniversary of the coronation of Queen Elizabeth II. Several pictures of the young queen in full regalia with her bejeweled crown and beautiful dress were displayed on the tables.

After breakfast Mom hurried back with Auntie and her six children to the boat's cabin where she gathered all her odds and ends, sweaters, underwear, towels, and such. She made separate bundles to be carried by each one of us. She went about this task expertly, almost mechanically. In her fourteen years of marriage, how many times had she packed and unpacked her things? She could not remember! It began in East Berlin with the news that the Russians were coming, then Austria, southern France, Paris, and now Canada. At first she had tried to save everything— her fur coat, silverware, tablecloths and wall decorations. Eventually she had learned to content herself with bare necessities. During these packing sessions, which she shared with Auntie, I was never allowed to help. I was in charge of my siblings. This was no easy task as the little ones cried, fought and giggled with excitement at the prospect of something new.

My youngest sister Beate had a fever. She wept a great deal. Mom forced her to swallow half an aspirin sweetened with sugar, but still disgusting, judging from the howls of the little girl. My little brother Joey pretended to be a plane and kept circling with his arms outspread, bumping into my little sisters, who protested with kicks and shouts.

After the immigration officials and health personnel had checked the passengers' passports and the custom officials had approved the luggage, everyone was allowed off the ship. Mom and Auntie gathered us together with our bundles and took us into a huge hangar with tables and benches. A group of charitable women welcomed us with coffee and tea. They spoke a peculiar French which we could barely understand. They were of limited help but directed us to the proper venues.

Mom's first concern was Dad. Had he sent her money? She went to the telegram booth and asked if there was a message. The attendants stared curiously at her foreign hairdo, her waist-long blond hair coiled in a chignon at the nape of her neck. They looked at each other and smiled. Mom ran frantically to various outlets; finally she managed to send a telegram to my dad to let him know we had arrived safely.

In the afternoon, Mom received my dad's money order for train tickets to Winnipeg. She cashed it and sighed with relief, counting the money over and over, bewildered by the strange bills bearing the British royalty figures and the unfamiliar coins bearing the heads of moose and beavers. Many of the coins were worn and she had trouble making them out. Also the size of the coins, so different from francs, confused her. Money always made my mother nervous.

The little ones began to whimper. They were hungry and thirsty. Mom wondered if the tap water was safe. In France tap water could not be trusted. But as she saw many people drink from the taps, she decided that this Canadian tap water would not kill us and allowed us to drink; however, to be on the safe side, she prayed all the while that we would not break out in a fever.

Afterwards, she went about the task of locating our train on the tracks outside the main station. We had to find a particular train for immigrants, which would take us to Winnipeg. Mom had dragged us to many train stations during our travels in Europe, but we never saw a sight as dismal and confusing as this railroad site in Quebec. All I remember is a huge dusty field with rails in all directions in the middle of nowhere. We were not allowed to board our train till later in the afternoon. Mom found some shade under maple trees and asked Auntie and the children to sit down on their bundles. Then she took me along to find a store.

There was a grocery store not far away. On the outside it looked like a turned over apple box. Inside, the victuals were piled along the walls up to the ceiling, and fresh fruit and vegetables were heaped upon a table. The proprietor spoke French-Canadian, a barbaric tongue to our Parisian trained ears. Mom asked for *pain*, bread. The grocer put several loaves wrapped in colorful plastic on the counter. *"Non, non,"* cried my mother. *"Je voudrais du pain!"* She looked around for the big brown loaves of crusty bread, so common in France, but saw none. "It's incredible," she told me in German. "This grocery store has no bread!" The grocer watched her with amusement. She must have looked very foreign with her worn out coat and blond chignon. "That's what you wanted: bread!" He pointed at the plastic wrappings. But Mom shook her head. I could see her blush nervously. She turned to me, her eyes full of tears, as if I could be of help.

A lady customer came in and looked at us curiously. She asked the grocer what was the matter. "This woman asks for bread, and then she says she does not want it." He sounded annoyed. The customer asked my mother in a gentle voice what she wanted. Mom explained that she was looking for regular loaves of bread. The woman pointed at the loaves of McGavin bread still lying on the counter. *"Non, non,"* cried Mom. *"Pas de gateau!* I would like bread!" My poor mom thought the loaves of bread were cake! "That's bread in Canada," explained the kind lady.

For the rest of her purchases Mom simply pointed at the food items she wanted. She bought six loaves of bread, a jar of jam, two bottles of milk, some apples and cheese. The grocer rang up the bill. After much hesitation Mom handed him a few dollar bills. He gave her change. Mom counted it carefully, turning the confusing coins over in her hands. One 25 cents was partly erased. She pulled me aside and whispered that she thought he was cheating her. She asked me to check the coin. I said that I thought the number 25 was written on it, although it was barely visible. Mom stared with bewilderment at the head of the moose. She pocketed her change. I helped her carry the merchandise back to the train station where Auntie and the children were waiting.

The children were not allowed to eat until we were all settled in the train. It was a wagon with wooden benches, especially reserved for immigrants. It would cross Canada from coast to coast and drop its passengers at their various destinations. The benches were uncomfortable, but the tired children would sleep on them anyway. They had often slept on benches during their hectic travels through Europe.

Finally the train started rolling. The children's eyes lit up. Even old Auntie chuckled. Mom opened the plastic wrappings of McGavin bread. Thin white slices rolled out. "The crook! I knew it! He sold me cake, not bread!" she gasped. She tasted a corner of a slice. "It tastes terrible," she said, then controlled her repugnance. Her children would have to eat it. "I wonder what it is?" she asked old Auntie, who agreed that this tasteless cardboard could not possibly be bread. The children were hungry. Mom went to work. She spread strawberry jam on the slices of bread and served them with milk. The children devoured the food with delight. Mom smiled. Whatever this white thing was, the children liked it.

When we entered Montreal, we stared with amazement at the huge illuminated cross on Mount Royal and the wide St. Lawrence River reflecting city lights. I was so tired I do not remember where we slept. The next day was gray and misty, but Mom insisted on making good use of our brief stay in the city. We quickly boarded a bus to the Oratory and climbed up the many steps to the basilica to view the panorama. Mom lit a candle at the shrine of Blessed Brother Andre whose special devotion to St. Joseph, she was sure, would assist us in our journey to meet Josef, our father.

Back on our train, we soon left the eastern towns and entered the countryside. Like many European children we were convinced that Canada was filled with aboriginals in feathers and war paint, and exotic animals like lumbering grizzlies, majestic moose, and stampeding buffalos. But instead we saw massive forests, huge lakes, endless fields, and a few lonely houses with red barns, very different from our European landscape of rolling green hills and picturesque villages. We thought we had landed in the wilderness. Miles and miles of wilderness! I stared out the window and felt cast away in an interminable ocean of meaningless space. I wondered why my dad had chosen this desolate land. For hours I watched streams, woods, fields, and telephone poles fleet by like in a monotonous reel.

Early one morning, we children ran to the window and shrieked with delight. A group of deer with their fawns was browsing by a forest stream, some of the lovely animals standing still like in a painting and observing us with moist eyes. Mom, and even old Auntie, came to the window and smiled.

We travelled for several days on what seemed an eternal journey. In the evenings we lay down on the hard wooden benches, which unfolded into beds. Mom and Auntie wrapped us in our coats to keep us warm. The clicking noise of the rails put us to sleep. At the train's longer stops, Mom hurried to replenish our food supply at nearby outlets. Mom was apprehensive. She worried about Dad. She wondered with Auntie if he would be at the station to meet us.

We children were still asleep on the hard benches when Mom and Auntie shook us awake with loud joyous shouts. "Hurry children! We are here!" They helped us into our coats and knapsacks and gathered our luggage.

But when we stepped on the platform of the train station, we did not see our dad. Mom and Auntie looked around in panic. Did something happen to him? A car accident or a fall? It was not possible that he had forgotten. Mom had telegrammed the exact date and time of our arrival. Disappointed and a little envious, we watched more fortunate passengers meet their connection and drive off in taxis and buses. Who could Mom ask? Where could she go?

"We better wait here," Mom said resolutely. "Josef knows we have arrived. He will find us. If he doesn't show up within an hour, I'll contact the hospital where he is working."

I sat down on one of our worn out suitcases and looked absent-mindedly at the trains chucking back and forth with metallic rumble and clatter. Mom held little Margie and Beate by the hand, and Auntie kept an eye on Joey and the twins, so that they would not approach the rails.

Mom saw my dad first. He was walking briskly our way with a big smile over his pale and tired face. We left our bundles and ran into his open arms, while Mom stood beside us, pink with joy. Even old Auntie, always so severe, took off her glasses to wipe away happy tears.

He had expected us at the main train station and was equally disturbed when he had not seen us disembark. After several inquiries he had found out that the train for immigrants had stopped at a platform further down the rails.

After a year of separation we were together again, ready to face the many challenges that immigrants face in a new country.

My dad opened a successful medical practice in Ponteix, a French Canadian community in Saskatchewan, where he could communicate in French most of the time. My little sister Ann, whom we had left with Mom's grand-parents in Germany, joined us a few years later. Unfortunately, we were not allowed to bring into Canada my handicapped brother Jean-Michel. Two other children were born in Canada – my brother Andre and my youngest sister Elizabeth.

Was the traumatic war forgotten? Regrettably, no. Its dreary shadow lurked for many years in our family like an unforgiving bitter ghost that claimed its victims. Eventually memories faded. Children married, new families were formed, and grandchildren came along. For the younger generations World War II was nothing more than a chapter in their history book.

On Remembrance Day, when I pin a red poppy on my lapel, I remember the many heartaches endured by families in the past and the sad blood shed by soldiers of all nations in those horrible times.

I sincerely pray in my heart that the world will never see the like again.

# Oma's True Stories

*Revised by Marguerite Courchene*

## How We Came to Canada

## Part I: From Germany to Austria (Berlin:1938-1945)

My mother, whom the grandchildren called Oma, loved to talk of my family's escape from Berlin and her difficulties in Europe before she came to Canada. She saw herself as a heroine who managed to overcome tremendous obstacles thanks to her unfailing courage and deep rooted faith.

"We could hear the Russians shoot in the east..." she would begin.

The date was late January or early February 1945. We were staying in an old farmhouse on a few acres bordering the Oder-Spree canal in Braunsdorf, a village east of Berlin. Dad, Josef Strohhofer, 41 years old, a medical doctor in Berlin, had purchased this small farm to shelter Mom and the children from the frequent air raids in the city. His aunt, Margaret Voit, called "Tante" lived with the family to help Mom with the children and the chores.

Mom, Erika Bartholme was 26 years old in 1945 and had given birth to five children in Germany: Erika (Marie) the eldest, in 1939, Joe (Volker) in 1940, Renée and Régine (Helga and Ute) in 1942 and Marguerite (Burgi) in 1943.

Dad, had to remain at his medical practice in the terrifying bombardments of Berlin. His duty to civilians exempted him from the military. Our former apartment on Mueller Street, where he had had his medical offices, had been razed to the ground by incendiary bombs. He had to move with his two unmarried sisters and helpers, Rete and Marie, and his office assistant Wilma to another building. He regularly listened to a clandestine British radio station to stay informed.

One night, he rushed by taxi, his usual mode of transportation, from Berlin to our house in Braunsdorf. He said to Mom, "The Russians are coming! Quickly, pack up. In the morning you are catching the last train out of Berlin."

"Where to?"

"South. Just out of this hell!"

Mom, with the help of Tante Voit, and Auntie Rete packed frantically essential items in suitcases and in the twin's baby carriage. Since it was winter and very cold, they packed the duvets, bed sheets, warm clothing, and cooking utensils as well as food for the trip.

Thus equipped, Mom, the five children and my two aunts were ready. A three feet tall wooden Madonna was packed carefully and devotedly in the duvet bedding. This Madonna accompanied us in all our journeys and remains a treasured family heirloom to this day. Mom attributed many miracles to her intercession.

Early in the morning, the sleepy children were settled on a horse and buggy headed for Fuerstenwalde, the city nearby. Auntie Rete sat in the buggy with the little ones and various bags. Mom (three months pregnant) followed on foot with the baby carriage filled with luggage. Tante Voit, who had grown up on her sister's Bavarian farm and was used to heavy work, lugged several heavy suitcases.

From Fuerstenwalde, the family traveled to Berlin where Dad was waiting at the train station to help us. He handed Mom a suitcase filled with the money he had saved over the years. He had gone to his bank in Berlin and had emptied his account shortly before all the German banks closed.

The train was so packed that people were holding on to railings on the steps. In desperation Dad simply pushed Mom, Auntie Rete and the five children into the crowded luggage wagon where people were packed like sardines.

Tante with the loaded baby carriage and heavy suitcases did not fit in. Luckily, another train was on its way. Mom called out to Tante that she would meet her in Munich at the train station near the air raid shelter. This was fortunate since all means of communication, including telephones, were disrupted.

The train stopped for half a day near Lake Constance because of bombing alarms. Mom and Auntie Rete went outside with the children to buy food and visit the lake. I remember the lake as soft and blue with a deserted sandy beach. Since no lights could be turned on with the danger of enemy planes overhead, night fell in total darkness. Mom and Auntie Rete felt their way to the train, terrified at the thought of losing one of the children. In the dark train, they reached out with their hands to count the heads. Luckily, the five little ones were with them.

Meanwhile, Tante Voit had arrived much earlier in Munich with another train that had not been delayed. She was very worried about finding us in the huge air raid shelter near the station. Holding on to the baby carriage and the luggage, she would desperately ask strangers if they had seen "a tall blond woman with five little children." Fortunately, she found us.

A few weeks earlier Dad had visited Duens, a mountain village in northern Austria, with a view of sending us eventually to this sheltered area. He had made arrangements with the town's mayor so we would be allowed to stay—Austria had been taken over by Germany much to the locals' resentment.

In Munich, Mom, our aunts and the children boarded the train to Feldkirch, a small town in Austria. It was winter and snowing. Our group of three women and five children started plodding along the snow filled road up to the mountain village, an impossible hike for the little ones. An obliging Austrian in a horse and carriage happened along, saw our predicament and gave us a ride to the village.

No lodging was awaiting us, so we stayed at the village's hotel for a few days, but this was impractical and costly. An elderly spinster offered her shabby small home to us. She was rather odd; it became obvious that we could not live there. Monica, another Austrian woman, invited us to stay in her house. She was neat and tidy and she was not pleased with so many noisy children. She had also promised her home to another German, Dr. Rabe and his family of twins, when they would arrive. So we had to find another place. Meanwhile, Auntie Rete, who could not tolerate the high altitude of the mountains, returned to her home in Straubing, Germany. Tante remained with us.

Mom told us that Dad managed to come to Austria to say good-by before he was enlisted. He had never held a gun in his life and was very nervous. He left with the dreadful knowledge that he might never return. Later, he reproached Mom bitterly for not having turned around to watch him walk away. I can imagine how distraught and lost Mom must have felt-- with five little ones, pregnant with a sixth, and her husband called to fight a losing war on the eastern front.

The parish priest offered us one floor of his spacious white house, located on a hill not far from the spired village church. The priest and his housekeeper had their bedrooms in the upper floor. One-year old Margie screamed at night. On one occasion the infuriated priest got up in the middle of the night, entered our bedrooms and gave her a good spanking. Mom was rather shocked by the behavior of this kindly priest.

Mom and Tante shared the kitchen with the priest's housekeeper. We children spent most of our days in the yard outside with strict orders to remain within limits, so we could be watched from the windows. Many refugees roamed about, and some Austrians disliked Germans.

Mom's child was due in August. She had received no news from my dad since he had been enlisted along with every able man, some as young as 15 and as old as 70. Many were killed in battle, taken prisoners or shipped off to labor camps — no one knew where or by whom. Around Easter Mom received a postcard with no return address and no signature, only the brief information that Dad had been taken prisoner. This gave her hope although she did not know his whereabouts.

To her surprise, Dad suddenly appeared on July 14, her birthday. We children were outside and frightened by the stranger. Mom was on the other side of the house hanging up laundry. She heard a familiar rasping, a clearing of the throat. She looked around the corner and thought to herself, "How odd! It sounds like Josef." To her immense joy, here he was!

We stayed in the priest's house for several months. At the end of August 1945, Beatrice , "Puppi" as Dad nicknamed her, was born. We were six noisy children now. We left the parish house and moved to the shabby upper floor of a farmhouse in the village. We had two rooms, one for my parents and the baby, and one for Tante and the children. Auntie did the chores and babysitting while Mom spent most of her time nursing the new baby. Dad indulged in the newly brewed cider at the village hotel and discussed politics with locals and other refugees. Many times he drank too much. Everything was so confused. Germans wanted to leave for other countries. But where would he find the money for three adults (Tante was a part of the family) and six children? Another doctor had left with his little family for Brazil. Dad had played with this notion, but due to lack of money or other reasons, he gave up this idea. To relax in the evenings, he played a card game called *Jassen* with Mom, Tante and another refugee, Dr. Rabe who had a wife and twins and who planned to go to America.

Mom told us that she had quite a bit of money hidden in her suitcase and was able to afford rent and food. When Dad arrived, he put the money into the local bank. After the war Austria abolished the use of the Mark and everyone was permitted to exchange a certain number of Marks for Schillings, the new Austrian currency. This included children. Dad was thus able to exchange a portion of his savings. In order to get more of his money exchanged, he offered a poor Austrian father of nine children one share, if he would exchange some of our father's marks for schillings. This man used our money gift to start the manufacture of clothespins and earn a living for his family.

Dad had his own incredible soldier story which Mom narrated in bits and pieces. In the confusion on the eastern front at the end of the war, younger troops simply dropped their guns and ran westward. Those who did not escape were taken prisoners by the Russians to be shipped by train to the dreaded Siberian labor camps.

Dad and other German troops were captured by the Russians somewhere in the east. They were made to sit down in rows in an outdoor make shift prisoners' camp. In the adjoining farm building, several Russian soldiers were celebrating their victory with vodka, songs and women. A tall thin man came out of the house, approached one of the drunken guards and whispered. Perhaps he was asking to borrow some prisoners for a task. As luck would have it, he beckoned to Dad to follow him out of the compound. That is how Dad escaped together with other prisoners. Dad ran out of sight and quickly discarded his military uniform—he was wearing civilian clothes underneath—and joined other escapees. They were very hungry and stopped at a farm for food. A woman gave them bread, but after they had left, she reported them. Somehow, Dad escaped again in the overall confusion. He did not know where he was. Perhaps Czechoslovakia. He only knew that he was heading south-west towards Bavaria. He crossed woods and frozen fields and munched on roots and anything edible he could dig up.

At one point he got hold of a bicycle. As he was resting in the forest with his eyes closed, two men approached him. One of them said, "Let's finish him off and take his bike." The other bent over him and said in a sad voice, "No. This poor guy might have a wife and children. Let's just take his bike." A narrow escape!

Dad came to a river near Germany. He did not know the river and he could not swim. American troops were crossing the bridge. He mingled with them. After they had crossed the bridge, they arrested him and took him to a make shift prison camp in the open air. It was bitterly cold and rainy. To get some rest, two men took turns holding up a coat or blanket while other men crouched underneath. Many got sick and died.

One day the Americans asked if there were any doctors among the prisoners. Dad was afraid and said nothing at first. When they asked for doctors again, he came forward. He was taken inside the Americans' quarters and treated very nicely. He had to give medical exams to prisoners about to be transferred or released. In July 1945, the

Americans let him go home. That is how he returned on Mom's birthday on July 14th.

# Part II:  From Austria to Southern France(1947-1952)

After the war Dad did not want to return to a dismantled and despairing Germany. His friend Otto Rabe was going with his wife and little twins to Los Angeles. Dad did not want to immigrate to the United States because he was concerned about some of their internal problems. However, he liked the idea of going overseas; so he joined his friend Dr Rabe in learning English with the aid of an outdated textbook. Sometimes, he would practice phrases like "I tickle thee" on us children and have us roll over with laughter. He had no idea that he would go to Canada later on.

With his medical practice in ruins and his money running out, Dad turned his eyes next door. France was recruiting laborers to rebuild their country. He applied to work as a laborer in France. The French board interviewed him, looked at his fine doctor's hands and rejected him at once with a terse "No!" Dad was furious. He decided to go to France on his own. He hired himself out as a farmhand in southern France. He had grown up on a farm in Straubing, Bavaria, but he had never worked on his parents' farm. His mother Maria (Tante's big sister) had insisted that her sons attend a private school and study at the University in Munich to take on a profession.

He amused us by telling us how he had poked oxen yoked to a plough with a long pointed stick and shouted "Hue! Hue!" like the local farmers. I always felt a little ashamed that he had done this menial job instead of using his talent as a doctor.

The plan was for Mom, who was pregnant with her seventh child, and the rest of us to join him in southern France near Tarbes.

Mom and Tante packed our luggage and moved to a refugee camp in Bregenz on the eastern edge of Lake Constance to get passports. The camp was dismal. We were crammed in bunk beds and provided with food tickets. Auntie had packed potatoes in large bags but some of our food was pilfered at the camp. While we children played in the courtyard of the compound, Mom agonized over the delays in the paperwork.

Since Dad had not been officially admitted as a recruited worker, he did not have permission to bring his family into France. This meant that Mom and the children were not eligible for a visa into France.

Mom insisted on joining her husband in France. When the assistants' refused to help her, she sat down stubbornly on a chair in the administration office and waited day after day. She watched the important administrators rush back and forth. As she would later tell us: "what else could I do?" One day, one of the administrators noticed her -- an attractive blond woman with a chignon and obviously very pregnant. He said, "I see you here every day. You should be near a hospital. Come into my office and let's talk about your problem."

Blushingly, she said in her broken French, "I want to join my husband. He is working in Tarbes."

"So, why aren't you there?"

"I can't get the papers— he didn't get to France as a recruited worker."

"How can I be of help?"

"He sent me this." She handed him a scrap of paper. "It says here that he is working in Tarbes." It was an unrelated document sent by Dad. It had some sort of stamp and Dad's undecipherable script. The sympathetic administrator wanted to know what the paper was about and to which address she would be going. Mom, inspired by desperation, replied that the document meant that Dad was a laborer for the French and had a house for us. Of course this was not true. The administrator was also concerned about the imminent arrival of the baby but Mom assured him she was only in her eighth month when actually she was overdue. The administrator confided, "I know how you feel. I too had to be separated from my wife for a while." He sat at his desk and filled out the forms that granted her a visa into France and said, "Take these to the secretary."

Mom did as she was told and waited the next days to be called over the loudspeakers to pick up her visa, but her name was not called. Disappointed, she resumed her daily wait in the office. On one of his pressing errands, the sympathetic administrator stopped with surprise: "Madame Strohhofer, why haven't you left yet?"

"I am waiting for my name to be called."

"But that was supposed to be settled! I'll see to it at once."

A few days later Mom received her visa; we were on our way to Southern France. But she suffered a shock. Tante was not issued a visa and could not accompany us. Mom lay down on her bunk bed and broke out in tears. How could she travel alone with a baby overdue and six small children? Tante would join us in France later, but that was of no help on this long trip.

Tante helped as best as she could. She helped Mom pack food and small items in little red rucksacks for the children to carry. Even the four year old twins, Helga and Ute (Renée and Régine), got their little rucksacks. My little brother Joey promptly fell and broke one of the bottles of sweetened tea in his bag. We always carried our drinks with us since tap water was unsafe. There were many diseases after the war such as polio, typhoid, and dysentery. At seven I was the eldest and the most responsible of the little ones. I was asked to carry an extra load. Annoyed at this injustice, I protested vehemently and threw my rucksack on the ground. Tante explained to me that she could not come with us; I had to be Mom's helper now. Tante noticed two young men who were taking the train to Paris with us. She gave them the meat we had packed, and pointing at my distressed pregnant mother, she said, ``Look after that woman!"

When we transferred trains in Paris to meet Dad in southern France, the two young men helped Mom with the luggage and the children since she was overdue and could not lift anything.

When we disembarked in Tarbes, Mom looked around for Dad. He was nowhere in sight. Full of dread with her labor cramps starting, she stood alone on the empty landing with her six children. Thoroughly worried, she left me in charge of my siblings and walked up a random road. What a relief when she finally saw him, walking towards her.

He took us children immediately to a hotel room in Tarbes and rushed Mom to the city hospital where she delivered a baby boy, Jean Michel in October 1947. The boy looked healthy but soon proved to be slow in development. After his birth, we visited Mom and the baby. We stayed in her hospital room overnight as she was alone in a room of empty beds. She hung her loaf of bread on a string, worried about rats. She could hear them squeal at night. Hospitals were still recovering from war time disruptions of services.

"Les Soeurs de la Charite", nuns with winged coifs, took care of refugee girls and orphans. Dad took us up the mountain to their convent in Bas-sur-Guerre near Lourdes. We did not know French and could not communicate. It was the first time we were away from our family. One day, I felt terribly abandoned and gathered my three little sisters around me (Beatrice, only two years old, remained with my parents) and told them in German that our parents had abandoned us. We wailed so loudly that the nuns came rushing out of the convent and put an end to our nonsense.

We were with the nuns in October and November 1947. It was pleasant almost every day. I took my little sisters on hikes in the nearby forest. With two small sticks I knit bits of wool the nuns had discarded. I learned from an older black girl how to use the silken threads of corn cobs to put hair on my stick dolls. I fed acorns on my outstretched hand to the little donkey that pulled the grocery cart up the hills.

My little brother Joe was sent to a boarding school for boys. When Mom and Dad visited him he had forgotten his German, and having not learned French yet, he was unable to communicate with them. Mom felt very bad about this.

My parents were making every effort to find a house for us. A peculiar but enthusiastic French lady, Madame Kaptekoum took Mom under her wing and helped her with the French language and local customs. Mom would mix up words like 'couteau'( a knife) and 'gateau'(a cake) and scandalize the visitors with her German manners. Best of all, this generous lady put Mom in touch with a proprietor who had a house for a reasonable rent in the village of Fontrailles. Finally,

Mom could bring her children home. I don't remember how we left the convent but I remember my joy when I suddenly saw Mom standing in the kitchen of our new home.

Our dad brought us to the house late at night. Perhaps, we had walked from the bus or train station in Trie, a distance of five kilometers. Perhaps, we had arrived in our neighbor's black automobile whose engine had to be cranked manually. In the five years we lived in Fontrailles, we often walked that route to Trie on various errands.

Tante Voit eventually was granted her visa and joined us in Fontrailles. She was of invaluable help to Mom. She would hack wood, clean, cook, garden and watch the children. Mom was soon pregnant again—this time with Annie, her eighth child. Dad did not stay with us but lived in a room in Paris where he studied at the Sorbonne in the hope of receiving his medical license to practice in France. He visited us several times during the year. He was often irritable and moody. He worried about his responsibilities to the family.

Within four months after our arrival in France, Mom's purse was empty. She had to wait two more months to be eligible for family allowance from the French government. She started sewing for the village people to earn some income. She had an old Singer machine with a foot pedal, and she used the living room as her drafting room. She continued this home business during our five year stay in Fontrailles. When I was home from my boarding school in Igon, I helped her hem and baste clothes for her clients and for us. She also visited elderly neighbors and advised expectant mothers; as a doctor's wife and mother of eight children, she was an expert indeed in this remote village without a doctor. ( In 2008 when my sister Margie visited the village, the neighbors still remembered the names of each family member.)

In those early days in France, Mom ran out of food. I remember that I was sometimes so hungry that my belly hurt. Tante would send us out of the kitchen and scold us for complaining. One day all the cupboards were bare: not a scrap of bread or a drop of milk anywhere. Mom had no choice but to send us off to school without lunch. She dreaded our return as she had no food for supper either. She paced about anxiously, trying to find a solution. Just then a lady customer came to her door to drop off some material for her boy's pants. My mother was sewing for the local people and was paid a modest sum after the garment was completed. This lady found my mom in great distress. Perhaps Mom was crying. The lady asked her why she was upset. Mom told her that school was almost over and that she had nothing for her children's supper. She did have potatoes in a garden plot nearby, but these were not ready to eat. The kind lady smiled. "You can dig up these little potatoes and cook them for supper. In a few weeks, everyone will have lots of big potatoes and you'll be able to buy them cheaply in the market." Mom's eyes lit up. She called Tante at once and had her dig up a pail of 'little potatoes'. These she cooked and served with shortening that remained in a jar she had brought from Austria. What a treat for her hungry children! Mom was convinced that a miracle brought that good woman to her door that very afternoon!

Mom persisted on her rights to a family allowance. She convinced the sympathetic government official in Trie to do the necessary paperwork with the argument that her husband had been in France for six months—the prerequisite for entitlement to a family allowance. The official arranged for her money to be paid at once, although she had only been in France for a couple of months.

In spite of the insecurity of Dad having no job and studying in Paris, Mom, Auntie and the children were fairly comfortable in the south. They managed on their own. They raised chickens and rabbits like the villagers. On Tuesdays they went to the farmers' market in Trie to sell chickens, eggs and rabbits, and to buy flour, bread and sugar. Mom continued her sewing business and Dad came back from Paris for short visits. He did a locum in Berlin once, but lost all his money when he tried to smuggle some medications through the French customs. He told us about the terrible conditions in Berlin and vowed again, never to take us back to Germany. He wanted to go to a country free from political upheavals and war. If he could not practice medicine in France, where would he go with so many mouths to feed? Frustrated, he returned to his boarding room in Paris.

Our family allowance, some modest help from German relatives, and pocket money from Mom's sewing, were sufficient for the family's needs. We never went hungry again. We ate lots of fruit, vegetables, legumes, jams and soups. We picked blackberries from hedges, plums, prunes, chestnuts and walnuts that fell on the ground, and hazelnuts and cherries our neighbors allowed us to pick. In the fall we helped with grape picking. Mom bought meters and meters of material and dressed us in matching dresses and coats. We also had magical moments thanks to Mom's imagination. She amused us with puppets made with potatoes and once even disguised herself as St. Nicholas.

Shortly after Anne was born, Mom was very sick with jaundice but recovered, thanks to a lot of rest and a herbal broth Auntie served her. We were eight children with Ann born at home on September 11, 1950.

Due to the limitations of the local schooling, Joey and I went to boarding schools; I(aged 10) was sent to a strict convent of the "Filles de la Croix" in Igon that trained me to become a nun; Joey (aged 9) went to a boys' school in Lannemezan. We both were model students, quiet and docile, with top marks. We came home for Easter, Christmas and the summer holidays. Letters and communication with parents were discouraged.

My little sisters attended the local one room schoolhouse across the road from our house, where the exuberant red-headed teacher Odette Fauque became Mom's lifelong friend. Odette was in her early thirties. She often left the classroom to look after her little son Jacques in her quarters next to the classroom. There are many happy anecdotes about our five years' stay in the sunny village of Fontrailles in southern France.

Meanwhile, Dad tried to find a way out of his dilemma. It was clear that he would not be able to take up a career in France. Someone mentioned that there were opportunities for doctors in Canada. Canada became his passion. He got a passport and left for a hospital in Winnipeg, Manitoba. After earning enough money for our passage by boat, much cheaper than travel by plane in those days, he came to fetch us to what would become our new country.

# Part III: From France to Canada (Paris 1952-1953)

Mom had a deep Catholic faith, which is quite extraordinary since her parents and siblings had not been religious. She believed that prayers to the Madonna had saved us in difficult times. In Paris, she turned again to prayer when we unexpectedly found ourselves in dire straits.

In the spring of 1952 we were ready to leave Fontrailles in southern France and set out for Canada. Mom, Tante and the children had passports and tickets for the boat. Dad, who had been working as an intern in a Winnipeg hospital, had flown back to Paris to accompany us on our long trip. With joy I left the dreary convent in Igon and returned to my family for this new adventure.

One early dawn in May, with glowworms still shining in the bushes, we were driven to the train station in Tarbes. Mom wanted to stop in Lourdes to pray to Our Lady of Lourdes at the famous grotto of St. Bernadette.

At our hotel in Lourdes Mom received a telegram from Dad, and her face turned white. Our Canadian visas were expiring in mid ocean before we would land in Canada; we would not be allowed to enter Canada without valid visas. The whole application process would have to be redone in Paris. Would we be on time for our boat? By plane we would have been there within a day and would have had no difficulties. We would also have been permitted to enter according to immigration law if our father had stayed in Canada to await our arrival. Unfortunately, he had left the country one month before the minimum six months required for residency status.

Mom and Tante prayed with desperate fervor at the grotto of Lourdes.

Quickly, we boarded our train to Paris but our spirits were low. I took offense at a pretty French would-be-model who ridiculed Mom for having produced children like a rabbit. I looked over at Tante, holding two year old Ann on her knees and showing her the setting red sun, and at Mom cuddling the little ones. My five year old little brother Jean Michel was dribbling a string of saliva and looking up with bewildered blue eyes. Mom and Auntie were observing him with worry.

In Paris, Dad ordered a car to wait for us in front of the Canadian Consulate so we would be on time for our boat, which was leaving from Cherbourg that evening. Dad was pale and stressed. Mom and Tante ushered us up the stairs to the Consulate office. We had to undergo a medical exam, for only people who were healthy and fit were permitted into Canada. The adults had passed the test. We, the eight children had to strip to the waist and line up according to age—a major embarrassment for me as my breasts were forming. The medical examiners approached us with charts and stethoscope, and asked us our name and age. They took X-rays of our chest behind a screen. When they came to five year old Jean Michel and asked his name in French, he was bewildered. He understood German, as Tante only spoke German, and he knew some French, but he could not speak. Confused, he suddenly started to howl. The authorities conferred with each other and cancelled our visas on the spot. They also cancelled Dad's visa because he was one month short of being a Canadian resident. The car that was to drive us to our boat left without us.

We were stranded in Paris – three adults and eight children with no money and no lodging. Our luggage was in Cherbourg where it was ready to be loaded on our ship. We had nothing with us.

Our parents took us to a subway entrance where Tante waited with us while they looked for a place to stay. The younger children clung to Auntie and cried loudly. People asked us if someone dear had died. Meanwhile, Dad contacted his former landlord in Paris and asked him if he could bring us to his hotel. When the landlord saw the eight young children, he said that there was no room at his hotel. He kindly offered us his small summer cottage in St. Denis, outside of Paris. We stayed there for a few weeks.

The water was *potable* that is, safe to drink. We children drank so much water that we were quite light headed. We looked for snails in the garden, for fun, not for food. Auntie cooked potatoes over a small petroleum burner. The potatoes were practically raw when we ate them. We lived mostly on meager rations of bread and jam. My shoes were too small and my heels bled, but this was the least of our worries.

Mom and Dad left us with Tante in St. Denis while they went daily by subway to visit specialists in the city to examine and re-examine our poor little brother. But the verdict was always the same. He was retarded in mental development. But Dad insisted that the boy was strong and fit, with potential for learning. Dad was going to pester the doctors and immigration officers till they gave us our visas. My parents did not want to spend the money they had saved for their boat trip to Canada, but eventually, they used some of it for our groceries.

On one of those desperate days, my parents went to St Germain des Prés to see a specialist. They were much too early for their appointment. Dad wanted to buy a coffee in a restaurant, but Mom spotted a church across the street. She said, "Let's stop there, and say a prayer!" They went into the church of St. Germain des Prés with Jean Michel. Mom prayed at a side altar of the Virgin Mary, beseeching her for help. A woman hobbling on crutches and wearing a grey cape approached her. It was Madame Van der Steene: a youthful fine face with a body crippled by muscular dystrophy. "Do you have a pencil?" she asked softly. "Somebody was supposed to meet me here at the altar but did not show up. I want to leave a message."

Mom searched her purse and gave her a pencil. The stranger looked at Jean Michel with curiosity. She asked the boy's name. "Jean Michel," said Mom. "Michel!" the lady cried out. "What a coincidence! I am gathering the names of boys named Michel. I will send their names to the Mont St. Michel as a special devotion to the archangel St. Michel."

Mom, attracted by her friendliness, confided her some of her troubles. Madame Van Steene promised to introduce my parents to a Madame Bernadac, a widow who owned a building on the Rue de Charonne and who might be of assistance. They were to meet her at a gathering of the *Croisés,* a club of altar boys, who were celebrating a special mass at Notre Dame Cathedral the following day.

This meeting was like a breath from heaven. Mom was convinced that the Virgin had granted her a miracle. Joey was an altar server at the mass in the beautiful gothic cathedral. After the mass my parents met Madame Bernadac, who informed them that she would rent them two rooms on the top floor of her five-floor building on the Rue de la Charonne, in the workers' district. This was at a time when it was almost impossible to find affordable lodging in Paris!

After her husband had been killed in the war, Madame Bernadac decided to use her wealth for philanthropic deeds. On the lower floors of her building she was running a kindergarten and a training school for young teachers. She also took under her wing a few mentally handicapped adults who helped in her kitchen.

One of the two rooms she offered us was a small white bedroom where my parents and the little ones slept. The other one, with unpainted cement walls, and previously used as a storage room, was large enough to accommodate two double beds for Auntie and the girls, a small bed for Joey, a long kitchen table and a small stove. The room was lit by two tall windows, which overlooked the courtyard, a stretch of a boulevard and the tall wall of the famous Père Lachaise Cemetery. We were sheltered for now. Mom and Auntie managed to give us adequate meals, buying sometimes end of the day products. We went to good schools and learned to speak Parisian French. On Sundays, when museums were free to the public, Mom marched us along the Seine to the Louvre, fancy parks and gothic cathedrals. I admired with Mom the beautiful Renaissance paintings and statues, while my younger siblings ran irreverently about, sometimes crying because they were thirsty after the long walks. This was 1952-53 when you could go up to the Mona Lisa and almost touch the famous canvas. On our way back, we watched sword swallowers, fire spitters and magicians on the *Place de la Bastille.*

In Paris, Mom had to reapply for Family Allowance, and this again involved another story of happy coincidences and good fortune.

A few months later, Madame Bernadac came with surprising news. She remembered that she had a cousin or relation who had a friend in the Canadian House of Commons. This friend might have been Ellen Fairclough, who would in 1958 become Minister of Citizenship and Immigration. Apparently, this lady took an interest in our situation and was ready to help us with our visa problems. Telegrams went back and forth between Paris and Ottawa. Almost immediately, Dad obtained his passport. He returned to his job in Winnipeg. But we could not go with him. We were not allowed to bring Jean Michel. Although born in France, Jean Michel was a German citizen and would have to return to Germany.

Mom asked her parents in Oberschefflenz, Baden-Wuertenberg, to help her out. They were willing to take him as long as they could have a 'healthy' child as well. Three year old Ann was chosen to stay with her brother in Germany, on the condition that she would join us in Canada when she was six years old, in time for school. I accompanied Mom on this train trip across the border and cried bitterly to leave my little brother behind, for we all loved him very much and I had a feeling that I would not see him again.

In fact, I saw him just before he died from a kidney disorder in Heidelberg at the age of 15. My grand-parents had put him in a special school. He had learned how to speak and was well liked in his village of Oberschefflenz where he helped farmers with small tasks. Dad had always hoped to bring him to Canada.

In Paris, another drama was unfolding. Beatrice had contracted scarlet fever and was hospitalized. Mom traveled every day by bus to visit her. Although still frail and pale, Beatrice came home just before we were due to leave for Canada.

After one year of difficulties and negotiations in Paris, we had our visas and tickets. Our ship, the Columbia of the Greek Line, was leaving Cherbourg in May 1953.

Mom almost missed our boat! She insisted on thanking the saints who had helped her. We stopped at Lisieux at the cathedral of *Sainte Thérèse*, the Little Flower. After watching a movie about the ascent of the Himalayas for our educational benefit, we boarded a bus to Mont St Michel, the famous island in the Atlantic. In those days, the island was only accessible during daylight. In the evening, the tide would isolate it from the mainland. In the cathedral was St. Michel's shrine, which Mrs Van der Steene had mentioned in connection with our Jean Michel in the miraculous encounter in the church in Paris.

We went to the monastery to find sleeping quarters. The abbots had at first offered us the pilgrims' quarters, which had not been used all winter. The bunks and mattresses were dusty and the walls covered with spider webs. Tante protested, and the monks kindly moved us to fine quarters reserved for visiting clergy.

Our second overnight stay was an accident. Mom did not know that the tide would shut the island off from the mainland. She had to wait till the next morning for the bus to take us over the open road. Our boat was leaving that day! Mom and Tante were trembling as the train progressed ever so slowly to our destination; they even had to change trains!

It was dark when we arrived in Cherbourg.. As soon as Mom was off the train, she raced to the docks, leaving Tante and the children behind. "When they see me, they will let us board!" she cried. The officers of the Greek Line sighed with relief: "Finally, you are here, Madame Strohhofer!" They had loaded her luggage and had been waiting for her all day!

A smaller boat took us to the ocean liner anchored further out. The crew served us a snack and showed us to our cabins. We were safely on our way to Canada at last.

We arrived in Quebec City in May. We boarded a special train for immigrants and arrived in Winnipeg where Dad was waiting for us. Again we did not see him at first because he had expected us at Winnipeg's main train station and did not know that we had arrived at a special platform for immigrants.

Dad was almost fifty years old and Mom was thirty five. I was thirteen and the eldest of eight siblings. In this new land two more children were born, André and Elisabeth.

We suffered the growing pains of many penniless immigrants, but pulled through with persistence, hard work and the help of kind people. Dad practiced medicine in Ponteix, Saskatchewan, for many years. My parents moved to Saskatoon, where all the children attended the University of Saskatchewan and took up various careers. Joe became a devoted priest in French Canadian communities. Most of the girls married and became teachers at schools and universities in several provinces.

Mom loved to tell and retell these episodes of hardship and courage as an example and encouragement to us. She wanted us to remember our family's past and be proud of our origins. She died peacefully at age 94, predeceased by Dad, who had died in a car accident in 1973. These stories are a cherished memory and an inspiration for our family, friends and anyone with similar experiences.

## Oma's Famous Christmas Stollen

500g flour

2tsp baking powder

200g sugar

salt

1tbsp vanilla

4 drops almond extract

1 tsp rum aroma

4 drops lemon flavor

1 pinch cardamom

1 pinch nutmeg

2 large eggs

125g butter

50g lard

250g very dry cottage cheese (must be crumbled fine like small
    beads)

125g currants

125g raisins

125g finely chopped walnuts or almonds

40g glazed lemon and orange mixed peels

50g butter to baste the top and sprinkle on 50g icing sugar

*Directions:* Put flour sifted with baking powder, salt and spices in a wide bowl or on a board. Make a well in the middle. On the outside edge, mix in the softened butter and lard with a cutting motion Put the sugar in the middle of the well. Break the eggs over the sugar and add in the vanilla, liquid extracts and flavors. Mix the sugar and these liquids in the center to form a dough. Add some flour as needed.

In the center of the well put the cottage cheese, and mix in with some flour. Also in the center, mix in the raisins, nuts and lemon peels. Cover everything with the flour mixture on the sides and knead quickly but gently to form a dough (add flour or water if needed).

On a lightly greased cookie sheet roll out the dough to about 1 in thickness. Baste on melted butter. Fold 1/3 of each side over the center to form a mound (size of a loaf). Baste top with butter. Bake at 350 degrees F for about 50-60 min. until golden brown. Tooth pick comes out clean. Sprinkle with icing sugar. Will keep several weeks if wrapped in aluminum foil.

# PHOTOGRAPHS

Dr. Josef Strohhofer with office assistants Wilma and Marie                    Berlin 1938

Berlin 1938.

Dr. Josef Strohhofer has just started his medical practice. His assistant Wilma and his sister Marie are assisting him in his busy office. He is full of optimism and wants to find a wife and start a family. The world is still at peace.

Berlin 1939

Just married to Erika Bartholme, Dr. Josef Strohhofer invites his aunt, Auntie Voit ("Tante") to join his household. Erika is pregnant with her first child. There are rumors of a war but all is still calm in Berlin.

BERLIN 1939 -Tante, Adolf, Erika, Rete

BERLIN ZOO 1940   Erika and Mother

Berlin 1940

Erika is visiting the zoo. There have been isolated bombings but everyone hopes the war will be over soon. People are restless but pursue their daily lives.

Berlin 1940

Berlin 1940

Mother takes Erika for an outing.  Her cousin Gisela Steltz takes the pictures.

Berlin 1940

Dr. Josef Strohhofer still hopes that the bombings will stop and that he will be able to continue his busy medical practice in Berlin. But in case things get worse he looks into a property in the quieter outskirts of the city.

Berlin 1941

Dr. Josef Strohhofer and his wife Erika take little Erika and Joe on an outing in the forest. It is quiet and restful outside of the city of Berlin where the nightly bombings cause fear and stress.

Berlin 1942

Erika is growing up.  She loves flowers.  Time for a picture.

Austria 1945

Berlin is about to be invaded by the Allies. Dr. Josef Strohhofer sends his family to a small village in Austria where they will be safe. Erika and her twin sisters enjoy the outdoors. It is Erika's first communion.

Austria 1945

Dr. Josef Strohhofer returns to his wife and six children after he is released from an American prisoners' camp. He does not want to return to a defeated and suffering Germany. He plans to take his family west.

Austria 1945

The Strohhofer children. Erika is holding the youngest child, Beate, born after her father's return from the war. The picture is taken in the yard of the priest's house where they are staying before finding other lodgings. The other children are Joey, the twins Helga (Renee) and Ute (Regine), and Margie.

France 1951

The family Strohhofer with Auntie ("Tante") stay in southern France for five years while Dr. Josef Strohhofer is looking for an opportunity to resume his medical practice. Erika and Joe are sent to boarding schools for their education. Here they came home for the Easter holidays. The youngest child is Ann.

Ponteix, Canada 1957

The family settles in Canada, where Dr. Strohhofer opens his country practice in Saskatchewan.

Two children, Andre and Elizabeth, are born in Canada.

MARIE SADRO

# Acknowledgements

With thanks to my friends and editors Margie Courchene, Linda Prystay, Elicia Prystay, Patricia Johnson, A. Strohhofer, the North Shore Writers' Association of North Vancouver, Dare To Be Heard of North Vancouver, the editors of Rogue Writers who published several stories in the NSWA anthologies, and many others. Many thanks also to Martin Crosbie and Karen Dodd, successful authors on Kindle Amazon, who encouraged me with my publication. Thanks also to my proof readers, Linda Prystay and Tricia Johnson who gave me some excellent suggestions.

MARIE SADRO

# Author's Notes

When the Berlin Wall fell, I decided to write down my memories of the old Berlin where I had spent the first years of my life.

I recalled with great emotion the images, feelings and people in my family as well as various childhood events. I added what my parents and relatives told me, although none of them wanted to dwell in detail on these terrible days. I combined these memories to create my stories, which are partly fictitious.

All my family members, my father, mother, relatives and siblings are as I remember them. Other non-family members are based on a variety of people who touched our lives. "I did not know you remembered all this," said my mother (Oma) who encouraged me to recall our past.

I wrote these stories for my children and grand- children so that they may know what brought us to Canada: a quest for peace. I also wished my readers to understand the terrible effects of war on innocent families and their children. I included Oma's stories, which are totally true, as she often reminded us in her life time. They are a tribute to her memory.

Some of my stories appeared in the North Shore Writers' yearly anthologies and in magazines. With the encouragement and help of friends and family members I edited them to produce my book *Erika: Stories*.

**Marie Sadro**
**Contact information**
Facebook: https://www.facebook.com/marie.sadro.1
Twitter: https://twitter.com/MSadro (Marie Sadro